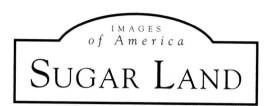

IMAGES
of America

SUGAR LAND

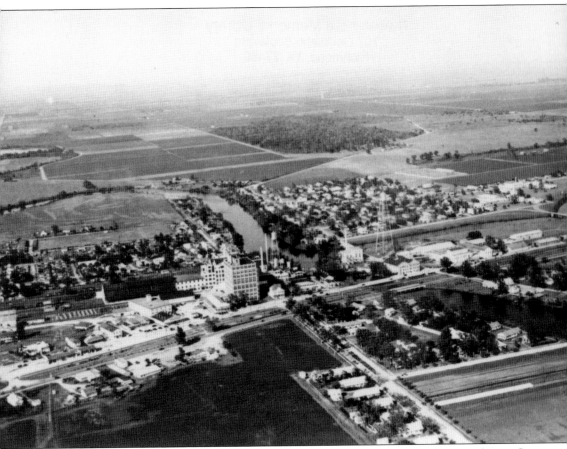

The company town of Sugar Land in Fort Bend County, Texas—home of Imperial Pure Cane Sugar and the Sugarland Industries—is shown around 1940. (City of Sugar Land.)

ON THE COVER: Before Sugar Land became a model company town attracting families, a refinery superintendent wrote that squalid conditions supported a population of "many ex-convicts and about every nationality anyone could mention. Sugar boilers, centrifugal operators, and other skilled [workers] were mostly from Louisiana. We never lacked for labor, and Sugar Land seemed to be the dump for deserters from ships in Galveston, hoboes needing a couple of bucks, and hikers." (City of Sugar Land.)

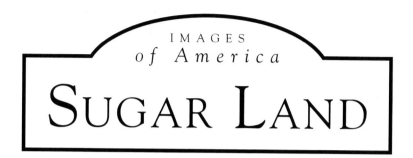

IMAGES *of America*

SUGAR LAND

The City of Sugar Land

ARCADIA
PUBLISHING

Published by Arcadia Publishing
Charleston, South Carolina

Printed in the United States of America

Library of Congress Control Number: 2009933146

For all general information, please contact Arcadia Publishing:
Telephone 843-853-2070
Fax 843-853-0044
E-mail sales@arcadiapublishing.com
For customer service and orders:
Toll-Free 1-888-313-2665

Visit us on the Internet at www.arcadiapublishing.com

This book is dedicated to the people of Sugar Land, whose leadership, vision, and pride have created a blueprint for a vibrant model city. Their guiding values are proudly etched into the city's public plaza for all to see: commerce, community, family, education, charity, faith, and hope.

CONTENTS

ACKNOWLEDGMENTS

The City of Sugar Land would like to thank the many people and organizations whose enthusiasm and commitment to document the town's past contributed to the creation of this book. Their goal was to capture the visionary spirit of pioneers, founding fathers, and entrepreneurs who successfully created a prosperous, idealistic company town that provided for the needs of its workers. This comprehensive approach to commerce and community led to the emergence of a master-planned city, one that continued to thrive and excel—a tribute to the community's earliest leaders, those who followed, and the many who endeavor to document their accomplishments.

Local historians Bruce Kelly and Jane Goodsill spent countless hours conducting oral interviews, researching written history, and acquiring photographs. They worked closely with the City of Sugar Land's Communications Department on the creation of this book.

Special thanks are extended to David Armstrong for allowing the use of content from his father's book; material from Robert Armstrong's *Sugar Land Texas and the Imperial Sugar Company* was instrumental in telling the story of early Sugar Land. Other information was obtained from The Texas Historical Association's *The Handbook of Texas*.

Unless otherwise indicated, a large majority of the photographs can be credited to the City of Sugar Land and the Sugar Land Heritage Foundation. Important contributions were also made by Leon and Bettye Anhaiser, Margery Brooks Ashford, Roger Bollinger, Tracey Matlage Calvert, Lupe Rodriguez Cavazos, the Fort Bend County Museum Association, Sybil Fowler, Muffett Guenther Gideon, Mayme Rachuig Hause, the Don "Doc" and Jenny Hull family, the Imperial Sugar Company, Jackie James, Chuck Kelly, Sally Rachuig Kelly, Gloria Laperouse Krehmeier, the Robert and Nona Laperouse family, former mayor Bill Little, the Clarence McLemore family, Jane McMeans, the George Morales family, Julia Moreno, Margaret Dierks Phillips, John Pirtle, Planned Community Developers, Ida Seitz Pokluda, Bob Roberts, the T. C. Rozelle family, Don Russell, Alfred Smallwood, Sugar Land Heritage Foundation, former Sugar Land police chief Ernest Taylor, the Texas Department of Criminal Justice, the Curley and Agnes Thomas family, Ernest Trevino, Minnie Ulrich, historian Diane Ware, and many more.

INTRODUCTION

Sugar Land is a city with a rich history, built by those with a tenacious spirit that seized opportunity and melded it with a commitment to quality and service to others. Its roots originate with the first 300 settlers brought to Texas in the 1820s by Stephen Fuller Austin, the "Father of Texas." The grant negotiated with the Mexican government allowed Austin to offer 4,605 acres to each family at a cost of 12.5¢ an acre. Rich land, water, abundant wildlife—and later the railroads—were critical in Sugar Land's development.

During the 16th century, Spanish explorers discovered a waterway stretching 840 miles from the northern Texas plains to the Gulf of Mexico. Named *Los Brazos del Dios* (the Arms of God), today it is known as the Brazos River. Native Karankawa Indians followed the Brazos, hunting and gathering food. Their remains have been unearthed near the Sugar Land Police Station on State Highway 6.

Austin's first colony extended from the Lavaca River on the west to the Trinity River on the east. The Gulf of Mexico served as its southern boundary, and the Old San Antonio Road, making its way from San Antonio to Nacogdoches, was the boundary on the north.

Austin chose five leagues of land for his personal homestead, which extended from present-day Harlem Road, east of Richmond, almost to Eldridge Road, just east of the Imperial Sugar refinery in Sugar Land. Each league was about a mile wide and extended from the Brazos River northward about 7 miles to include the fertile Oyster Creek watershed. Modern-day Sugar Land is within the prime real estate Austin chose for himself.

Austin decided to settle in San Felipe, relinquishing his leagues to others—Jane Wilkins, Jesse Cartwright, Mills Battle, and Alexander Hodge. The fifth and eastern-most league, where the company town of Sugar Land developed, went to Samuel May Williams.

Williams never lived there. He instead settled in Galveston in 1837 and sold the league to his brother Nathaniel in 1838. Another brother, Matthew, managed the plantation for Nathaniel, making his home there and calling it Oakland Plantation. Within a few years, the market for sugarcane increased. In 1843, Matthew installed a mill to grind his cane on the same site where the Imperial Sugar refinery now stands.

Samuel and Nathaniel sold the property after Matthew died in 1852. Two Brazoria landowners, Benjamin Franklin Terry and William Jefferson Kyle, purchased the land.

Terry and Kyle immediately renamed the area Sugar Land. They increased the size of their holdings by buying up adjoining plantations. Their 12,500-acre Sugar Land plantation became one of the largest in Texas. They convinced the owners of the Buffalo Bayou, Brazos, and Colorado Railway (BBB&C) to bend their tracks past their sugar mill and cotton gin, a major accomplishment credited for the future growth of Sugar Land.

In August 1861, Terry departed his beloved Sugar Land to lead the Confederate regiment called Terry's Texas Rangers. Colonel Terry was killed leading his first charge near Woodsonville, Kentucky, the place where he had been born 40 years prior. A large funeral ceremony, attended by dignitaries throughout the state, took place in Sugar Land.

Kyle died in 1864 at age 61, apparently worn out from the effects of the war. His brother Robert managed the property for the Kyle and Terry heirs.

The government appropriated the cotton crop of 1865. Planters were not able to raise a crop the following year. Productivity came to a virtual halt, and land values declined dramatically. Many landowners abandoned their properties or sold them for as low as 20¢ on the dollar. However, the Kyle and Terry Plantation survived the downturn.

Col. Littleberry Ambrose Ellis began acquiring acreage just west of the Terry and Kyle Plantation in 1868. Col. Edward Hall Cunningham entered into a partnership with him in 1875 to bring the state's convict lease system to Ellis's 5,300-acre plantation, Sartartia.

Cunningham began purchasing the neighboring Terry and Kyle properties and joined with Ellis to build a 600-ton raw sugar mill near the intersection of today's U.S. Highway 90A and Texas 6. Called the Imperial Mill, it was operated with leased convicts.

In the 1890s, Cunningham constructed the first sugar refinery in Texas to process the thousands of acres of cane harvested on his vast acreage. He became known as the "Texas Sugar King." He added convict quarters just north and adjacent to his mill and refinery in the horseshoe bend of Oyster Creek.

Cunningham had increased his holdings to 12,500 acres and built a railroad and a semblance of a town, where mostly drifters, vagrants, and sailors off Galveston ships sought work during the short sugarcane harvesting and crushing season.

By 1903, Cunningham suffered a series of setbacks, eventually placing his Sugar Land holdings into receivership. Refinery construction was delayed when part of his heavy machinery was lost at sea. Then severe floods in 1898 and 1899 destroyed crops and damaged property and a three-story boiling house burned down. Next, the Great Storm of 1900 ripped through the area wreaking havoc and destruction. Once the refinery was up and running, he began importing raw sugar from Cuba to operate it year round, but lacked sufficient credit to continue the practice. The aging Cunningham would never recover financially.

Meanwhile, Isaac Herbert Kempner Sr. (Ike Kempner), of Galveston, and William Thomas Eldridge (W. T. Eldridge), of Eagle Lake, partnered in 1905 to form the Imperial Sugar Company. Their purpose was to purchase Ellis's neighboring Sartartia Plantation. At the time, Gov. Thomas M. Campbell was in the process of centralizing the state's prison system and phasing out the convict lease system. His desire was to purchase the Ellis and Cunningham properties to create a special prison unit that would provide foodstuffs and other goods contributing to the self-sufficiency of the statewide prison system.

After lengthy negotiations, an agreement was reached that Kempner and Eldridge would sell the Sartartia Plantation to the state. In return, Kempner and Eldridge would acquire the failing Cunningham properties and guarantee the state a minimum $3 per ton for the prison's cane harvest.

Soon after the start of the 20th century, the partners began in earnest to design neighborhoods for workers and their families. The Quarters, later renamed Mayfield Park, and The Hill already had homes. They built streets, added more houses, and created two other neighborhoods—Imperial Boulevard and The Flats.

Kempner and Eldridge practiced a business model known as welfare capitalism, providing an environment and amenities for workers and their families, neither required by law nor benefiting their industry. A first-class school was built in 1918 and enlarged in 1931, a symbol of their commitment to nurture workers' children instead of exploiting them. That strong vision, commitment, and foundation for Imperial Sugar and its company town were established by Ike Kempner and W. T. Eldridge. It lasted more than nine decades carried on by Ike's sons, first Herbert and then Harris, drawing to a close with his grandchildren.

By the mid-1950s, the world was changing, and Kempner realized Sugar Land's survival was dependent on incorporation, a move intended to wean the town from his beneficent rule. On December 29, 1959, the City of Sugar Land was born.

One

EARLY YEARS

The early years of Sugar Land's history play an integral role in its evolution. Originally, Stephen F. Austin planned on parceling out his colony in square-mile segments, but the Spanish government required settlers receive much larger tracts of land—a league and a labor—totaling about 7 square miles. This early decision by Spain to grant larger parcels of land to the early settlers has greatly influenced the unusual growth and development of Sugar Land.

Each landowner from Austin to partners W. T. Eldridge and Ike Kempner either kept their leagues intact or added to them by purchasing neighboring plantations. By the time Eldridge and Kempner acquired the small company town of Sugar Land and its surrounding acreage in 1908, the property had grown to almost 20 square miles.

Over time, each plantation owner contributed to the economic success and improvement of the property, allowing the vast property to stay intact. The Williams brothers built the first sugar mill in 1843. A decade later, Benjamin F. Terry and William J. Kyle influenced the railroad to run past their sugar mill and cotton gin and improved planting, harvesting, and transportation methods. Col. Edward H. Cunningham built the first sugar refinery in the late 1800s and reached distant markets by connecting to the long-haul railroads with the Sugar Land Railway.

The stage was set in 1908 for partners Eldridge and Kempner to create a model company town that would eventually evolve into an incorporated city and flesh out the vast acreage kept intact until 1972 when the Kempner family sold 7,500 acres to Gerald Hines Interest for the development of First Colony.

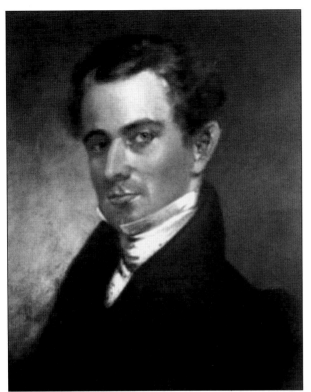

Stephen Fuller Austin (1793–1836), widely considered the "Father of Texas," fulfilled the contract of his deceased father, Moses Austin, by bringing 300 families to colonize Texas on behalf of the Mexican government. Granted the equivalent of 13 present-day Texas counties, he chose five leagues in the Brazos River and Oyster Creek watersheds for his personal homestead, the area where much of Sugar Land is located today. (The Dolph Briscoe Center for American History, University of Texas at Austin.)

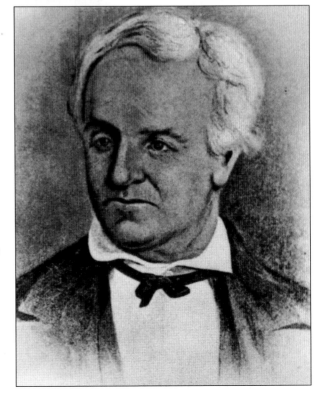

A Rhode Island native, Samuel May Williams (1795–1858), was Stephen F. Austin's secretary, wrote deeds in Spanish, kept records, and directed colonial affairs during Austin's absences. He received 11 leagues in Austin's colony, one of which is part of Sugar Land today. He was instrumental in founding the Texas banking system and secured financing for the Texas Revolution in 1836.

Benjamin Franklin Terry (1821–1861) was elected to the Texas secession legislature in 1861 to represent Fort Bend County. He helped organize Terry's Texas Rangers for the Confederacy and was killed during their first battle December 1861 in Woodville, Kentucky. Originally buried in Sugar Land, he was reinterred at Glenwood Cemetery in Houston in 1880. (The Dolph Briscoe Center for American History, University of Texas at Austin.)

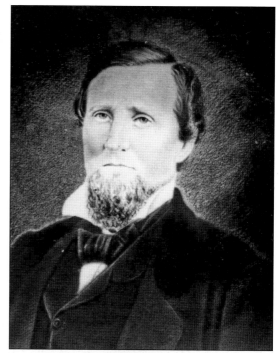

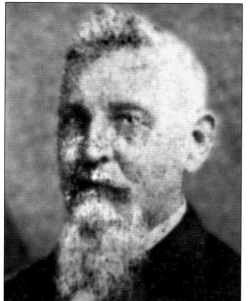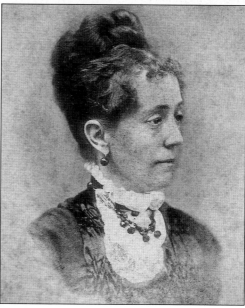

Col. Littleberry Ambrose Ellis, a Mississippi native (left), became a major landowner in Sugar Land after the Civil War. His grandfather, Ambrose Ellis, and uncle, Richard Ellis, signed the Texas Declaration of Independence in 1836. Littleberry served in Hood's 4th Brigade during the Civil War. Afterward, using convict labor, he established a large plantation encompassing the area of today's Central One Unit of the Texas Department of Criminal Justice and named it after his daughter Sartartia (right). Littleberry also renamed the depot on his property for Sartartia. The two-story frame building housed a post office and general store with a hall above that hosted Saturday night dances and Sunday church gatherings. (Roger Bollinger Collection.)

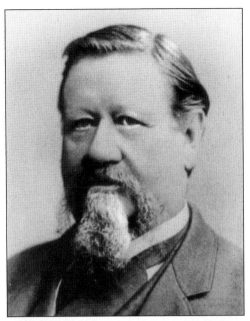

Col. Edward Hall Cunningham, an Arkansas native and San Antonio businessman, organized the Mustang Grays in Hood's 4th Brigade during the Civil War and was wounded 14 times. He purchased acreage at Sugar Land after the war, used convict labor on his plantation, and provided them quarters north of the refinery within a horseshoe bend of Oyster Creek. In 1896, Cunningham spent $1.5 million building the first sugar refinery in Texas.

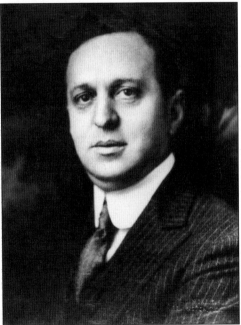

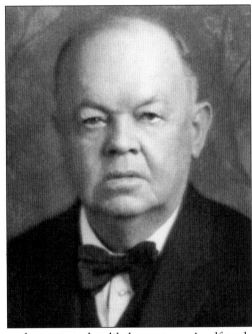

Ike Kempner (left) and W. T. Eldridge (right) may have seemed unlikely partners. A self-made man, Eldridge left home at age 12, picked cotton, eventually became a sheriff, owned a mercantile business and railroad in Eagle Lake, and successfully operated two company towns, Eldridge and Bonus. In partnership with Kempner, he became general manager of their Sugar Land enterprises. Born in Ohio and raised in Galveston, Kempner attended Virginia's Washington and Lee University. The oldest of 11, he was just 21 when he took over the family enterprises upon his father's death in 1894. Kempner expanded the family interests to banking and insurance, founded Imperial Sugar and Sugarland Industries, and spearheaded rebuilding Galveston after the devastating 1900 hurricane.

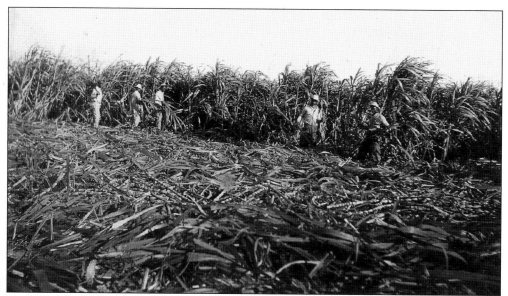

Harvested from October to December, sugarcane was hand cut, the leaves were stripped from the stalks, and the cane was then crushed. One-third of the harvested stalks were saved for seed cane. A field was replanted every three years by laying the cane stalks horizontally and lightly covering them with dirt. New stalks readily sprouted from the nodes of the planted cane stalk.

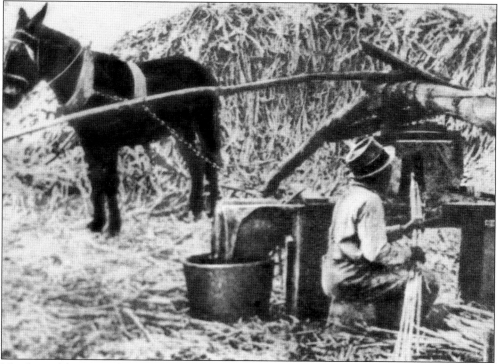

Members of Austin's colony brought sugarcane stalks with them to plant in Texas. They discovered this plant flourished in the rich soil of the Brazos River and Oyster Creek watersheds. In the field, cane juice was obtained by crushing the stalks. Pictured here is a mule-powered cane sugar crusher used in the early days to extract cane juice.

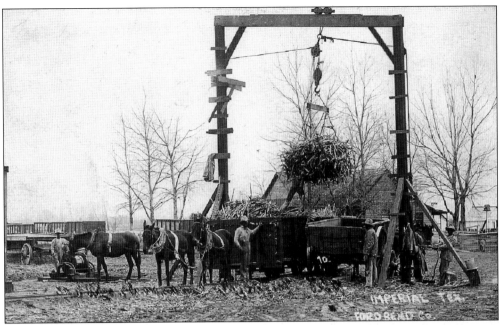

Transporting cane to the mill for processing was a demanding job. As the quantity of cane increased, narrow-gauge railcars transported the harvest to the mill. Hoists were used to lift the cane into the railcars, as the convicts transferring cane from a wagon to the railcar in the above photograph illustrate. Crews moved portable tracks from field to field to facilitate loading. The picture below shows a long train of mule-powered railcars hauling newly harvested cane to the nearest mill. These pictures were taken on the Imperial Farm, once owned by Kempner and Eldridge. Later sold to the State of Texas, it became part of the Texas prison system.

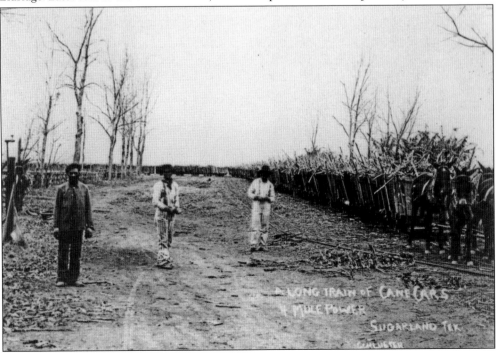

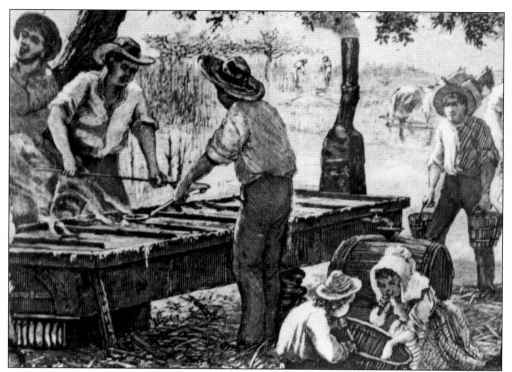

Pictured is a typical sugar-boiling process using an early open kettle. The juice was boiled in iron kettles or troughs until it became brown, sticky crystals. As the cane juice continued to boil off the water, amber sugar crystals formed.

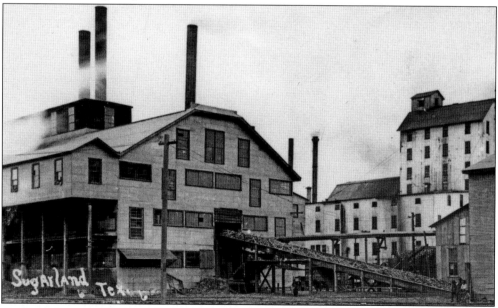

At the raw sugar mill, cane stalks were placed on a conveyor belt and transported into a building where crushers separated the juice from the fiber. For best sugar content, cane stalks had to be processed within three to five days, although cold weather also helped retard the loss of sugar levels. After the moisture was removed, the raw sugar crystals formed.

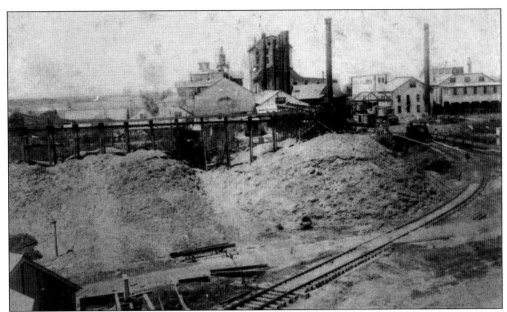

The dry, fibrous cane residue left after crushing is called bagasse. It was transported across Oyster Creek on an elevated conveyor belt and dumped into large piles on the northwest corner of present-day Main and Kempner Streets. Bagasse was burned as fuel to generate power for the mill and was also used to make paper.

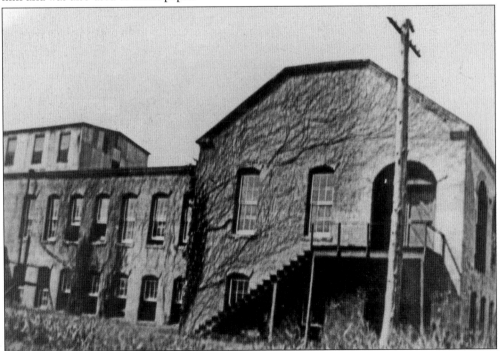

A paper mill built during the ownership of E. H. Cunningham operated until sugarcane production ceased. The paper mill faced present-day U.S. Highway 90A, east of Main Street. In later years, the mill housed various entities, such as a printing shop, storage area, and offices; the upstairs was a community hall.

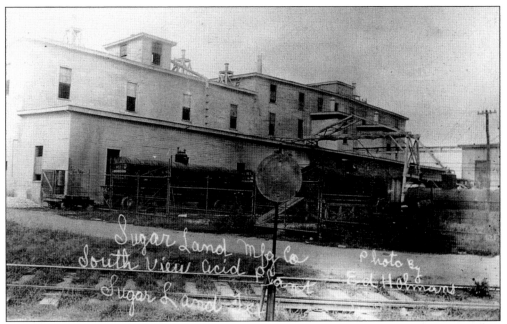

Cunningham also produced sulfuric acid for use in making paper. The acid plant was north of the paper mill, near where the present-day water tower stands. Battery acid was produced, as were weaker acids, such as vinegar, which were used at the nearby canning plant. The acid plant was torn down before 1924.

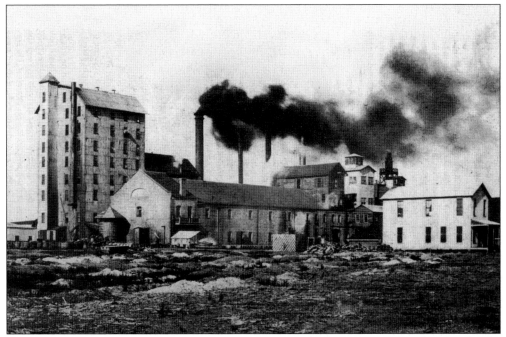

In the early 1890s, Cunningham recognized a significant new industrial trend: free-flowing granular white sugar. He began construction of a cane sugar refinery at Sugar Land to manufacture 100,000 pounds per day of the refined white-grained sugar. Pictured is the refinery as it appeared around 1895—the first sugar refinery in Texas.

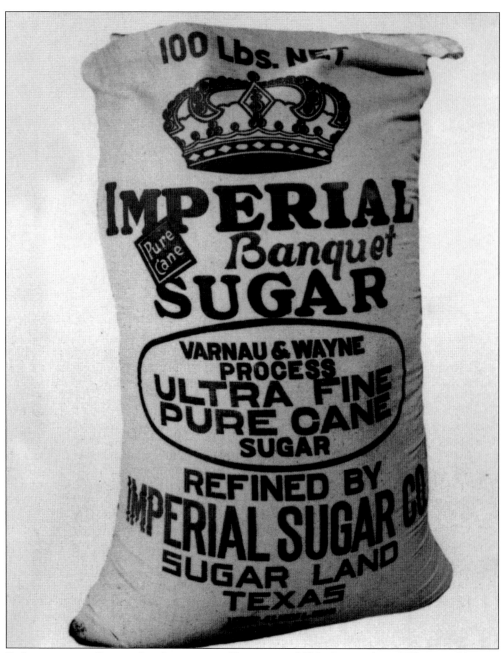

Before acquiring Cunningham's properties, Kempner and Eldridge purchased Ellis's neighboring Sartartia Plantation and the Imperial (sugar) Mill. They named their partnership the Imperial Sugar Company after the Imperial Hotel in New York City, adopting the hotel's crown logo as the symbol of their new business. Over time, Imperial used five different crown designs. The City of Sugar Land includes a crown as part of its official logo today.

Two

RAILROADS

Early Texas transportation was beset with obstacles. Dirt roads became impassible during rain or floods, and travel along the Brazos River was often impossible due to high or low water levels. During the Republic of Texas and early statehood years, river improvements, canals, and plank roads were proposed, but rail expansion emerged as the winner.

In 1853, the Buffalo Bayou, Brazos, and Colorado Railway (BBB&C) became the first to operate in Texas and the second west of the Mississippi. Its initial 20-mile segment reached from Harrisburg (Houston) to Stafford's Point (Stafford). The BBB&C eventually expanded an additional 12 miles west along the Old Spanish Trail (U.S. Highway 90A). The original plan was a straight line from Stafford's Point to Richmond; however, Sugar Land plantation owners Benjamin Franklin Terry and William Jefferson Kyle convinced railroad owners to bend the rail line past their sugar mill and cotton gin located at the present-day Imperial refinery. Their offer of 2,500 acres of right-of-way valued at $250,000 was hard for the railroad to refuse.

In 1893 and 1894, Col. Edward Hall Cunningham built the Sugar Land Railway connecting his new sugar refinery to the Santa Fe and International and Great Northern Railways at junctions near Arcola. He hauled products from his sugar mill and paper mill, as well as cotton, corn, and other crops. In 1902, Cunningham shipped his first cargo of raw Cuban sugar from Galveston to Sugar Land.

In 1907, Sartartia Plantation owners Ike Kempner and W. T. Eldridge chartered the narrow-gauge Imperial Valley Railway. Tracks were built through their plantation, and they later acquired the Cunningham properties and merged it with the Sugar Land Railway by 1908. They increased its tonnage by bringing in raw sugar and sending out a refined product. Besides passengers, also transported by rail were livestock, farm produce, and manufactured items from Sugar Land's paper mill, acid plant, cotton gin, feed mill, meatpacking plant, potato dehydrating plant, and mattress company.

By 1926, Eldridge sold the railroad to Missouri Pacific, which continued hauling raw sugar inland through the early 1970s, when its tracks were abandoned and removed.

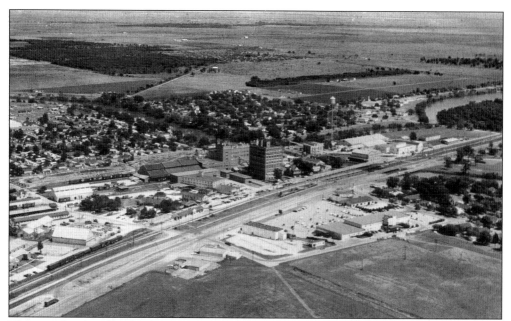

This aerial view of mid-1950s Sugar Land shows the apex of the BBB&C's bend passing the Imperial refinery, where the Terry and Kyle sugar mill and cotton gin were located in 1853. Over time, as rail lines consolidated from the East Coast to the West, it became the Southern Pacific Railroad. Today the track is the Missouri Pacific Railroad's busy main line from the Port of Houston to western destinations.

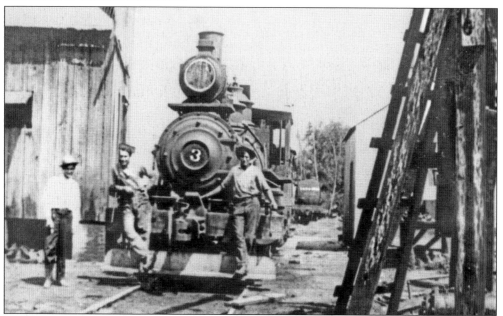

Railroad workers pose at the Sugar Land Railway roundhouse. Cunningham completed 14 miles of track, forming connections with the Santa Fe Railroad at Duke, Texas, and with the International and Great Northern Railroad (later known as the Missouri Pacific Railroad) at Arcola, Texas. He was able to ship to most destinations in the central United States from his Sugar Land interests and demand competitive prices and service from the long-haul railroads.

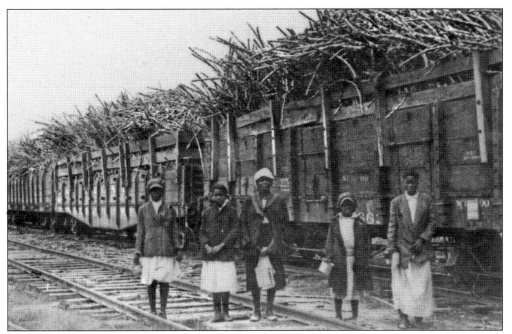

Workers stand in front of railcars loaded with fresh-cut cane. In addition to long hauls, the Sugar Land Railway transported fresh-cut cane from neighboring plantations south of Sugar Land. Tenant farmers participated in the backbreaking work of planting, cultivating, and harvesting cane as well as loading it into railcars.

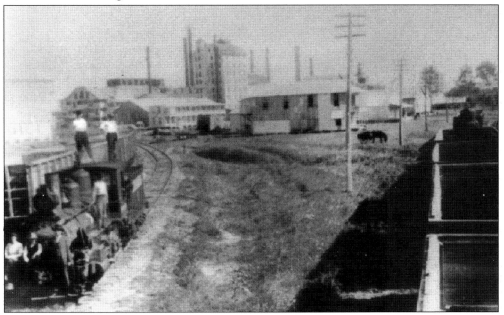

The tall building in the background is Texas's first sugar refinery built by the "Texas Sugar King," Edward H. Cunningham. It sat about 50 yards north of the Galveston, Harrisburg, and San Antonio Railroad on the right, now the Missouri Pacific Railroad. The train on the left is the narrow-gauge Imperial Valley Railway connecting the mill and refinery to the neighboring Sartartia Plantation, later reaching the Foster Farms north of Rosenberg.

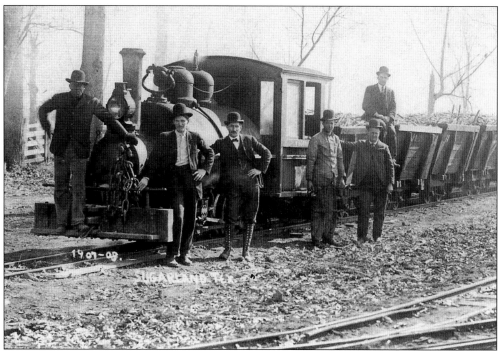

Imperial Valley Railway workers show off their locomotive and load of cane in August 1907, soon after the company's charter on May 30 of the same year. The railway was projected to extend from Sugar Land northwest along the east valley of the Brazos River to a junction with the Houston and Texas Central Railroad near Hempstead in Waller County, a distance of 60 miles.

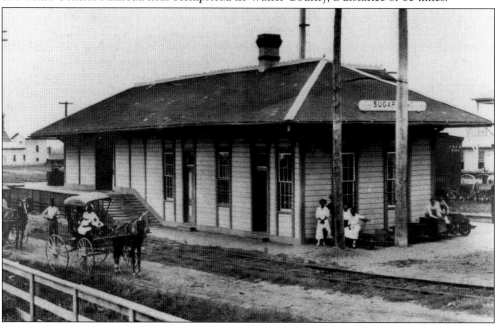

The Southern Pacific Railroad built its first Sugar Land depot in 1903. Harris Kempner, Ike Kempner's son, recalling a visit to Sugar Land with his father in 1911, remarked, "It was necessary to let down the gate at the Sugar Land junction, and we would hastily disembark at this unscheduled stop."

Three

BIRTH OF THE COMPANY TOWN

Col. Edward Hall Cunningham's deteriorating small company town was not unlike many others in the United States near the beginning of the 20th century. Ike Kempner and W. T. Eldridge began a process of transforming Cunningham's Sugar Land into a model company town. They acquired Cunningham's property in 1908. At the time, Texas governor Thomas Campbell was campaigning to clean up the state's convict lease system. To accomplish this, he proposed the state buy Kempner's and Eldridge's Sartartia Plantation, as well as the adjoining Cunningham properties.

Kempner and Eldridge worked out a deal to exchange the Sartartia Plantation for the Cunningham properties, guaranteeing a minimum $3 per ton for the state's sugarcane crop. As a result, the Sartartia Plantation became Texas's Central Prison Unit. Cunningham's vast acreage—with a refinery and a seedling town—suited both Kempner and Eldridge. Kempner could practice his vision of welfare capitalism, whereas Eldridge could use his entrepreneurial experience to oversee businesses, manage large acreages, and build a company town.

They went about cleaning up what some called the "Hell Hole of the Brazos"—a small, run-down, isolated industrial center that included a raw sugar mill, refinery, paper and acid plants, a commissary, saloon, and pool hall. A neighboring bar and brothel were immediately closed, and Cunningham's convict population was moved from the refinery property to the Sartartia Plantation they had recently sold to the Texas State Penitentiary System.

Partners Kempner and Eldridge were set to launch a five-decade transformation of the company town of Sugar Land, the precursor of today's vibrant city.

Employing Kempner's vision to create a model company town, Eldridge managed the refinery and built streets, houses, commercial businesses, churches, schools, and medical facilities to draw "family-type" workers to their isolated refinery and town. A capitalist venture, it also took workers' needs into consideration. The company's long employee tenures and Sugar Land's successful evolution from company town to dynamic incorporated city testify to their adherence to this concept. Sugar Land was in stark contrast to many company towns where family exploitation, shoddy infrastructure, and poor living conditions led to the demise of the community.

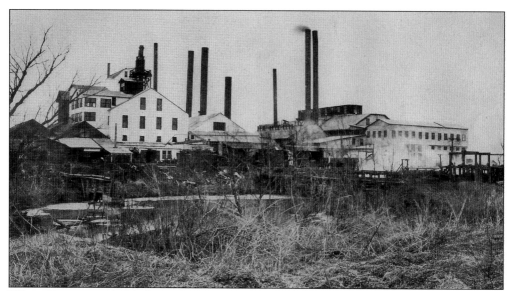

When Kempner and Eldridge acquired Cunningham's deteriorating refinery in 1908, they were faced with a decision to either improve the refinery or create a functioning company town. Determined to do both, they practiced what today is known as "delayed gratification." Harris Kempner, Ike's son, recalled, "All the earnings were plowed back [into the endeavor] for many years while stockholders waited for the dividends on their investments."

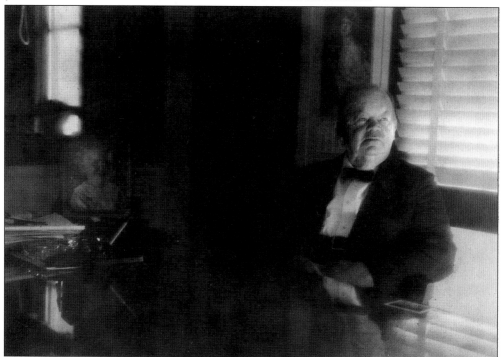

Eldridge made Kempner's experiment a reality. A rugged individualist, he started out as a farm laborer and eventually owned railroads and even operated a bank. Although he made news for killing two men, one a business partner, his legacy is the creation and development of the successful company town of Sugar Land.

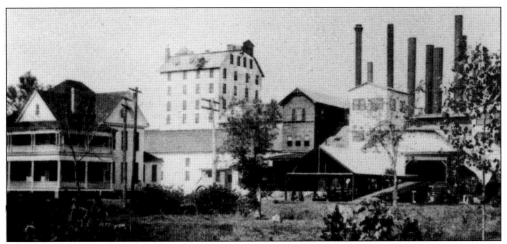

Eldridge lived in the Victorian house on the left, originally the home of Littleberry Ellis at Sartartia. Eldridge literally positioned himself as a hands-on manager by moving the house, by rail, from a mile west of town to the refinery property, where it would serve as both his home and office. He installed Sugar Land's first telephone line from his house to the refinery, maintaining contact with supervisors at all times.

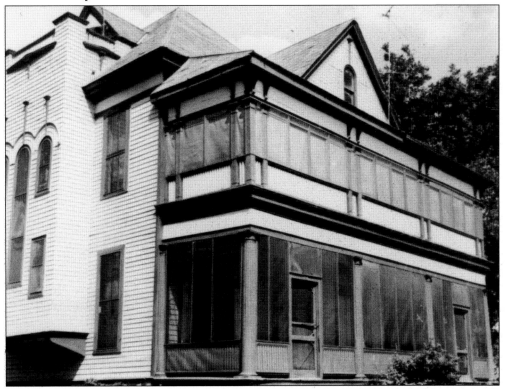

Eldridge's refinery home was built decades earlier by leased convicts who expertly fastened it with wooden pegs. From there he involved himself in every aspect of the town's business. Kempner eulogized Eldridge, stating, "His education was largely in the school of experience, which taught him practical lessons of construction and development that contributed greatly to a thoroughness of mentality and a rugged sense of honor."

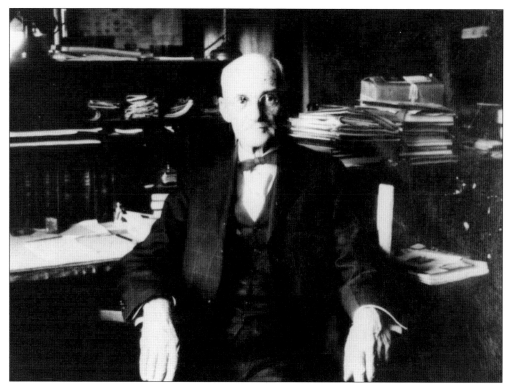

M. R. Wood came to Sugar Land in 1901 as Cunningham's chief chemist and engineer. In 1925, he praised Eldridge's and Kempner's accomplishments by contrasting them to Sugar Land's prior squalid conditions: "Twenty years ago this place was known as the 'Hell Hole of the Brazos.' That was before Eldridge and Kempner took charge; when there was little here but a convict camp and a dinky refinery."

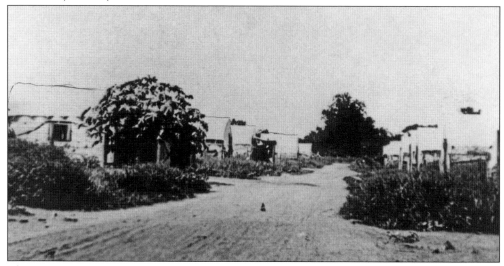

These primitive canvas-roofed houses inherited from the Cunningham era did not fit the partners' idea of attractive housing. Eldridge began his campaign to improve worker conditions, transforming the town from a primitive camp for seasonal, transient workers to an attractive place for individuals to take root with their families, which developed a permanent, reliable workforce.

Gus Ulrich, at age 26, assisted Eldridge on the neighboring Sartartia Plantation, soon becoming Eldridge's right-hand man. He was instrumental in not only attracting refinery workers but also skilled carpenters, craftsmen, storekeepers, and tenant farmers, many of whom came from the Schulenberg and Flatonia area where he previously lived. In fact, the influx from there was so great, Sugar Land became known as "Little Schulenberg." By 1917, Ulrich and his crews built 400 homes for a population of 1,200 people.

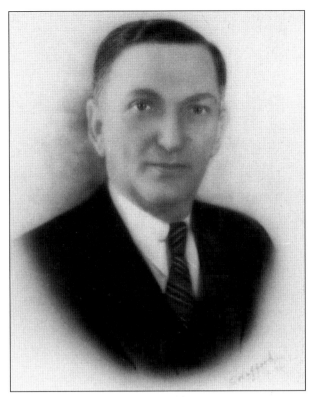

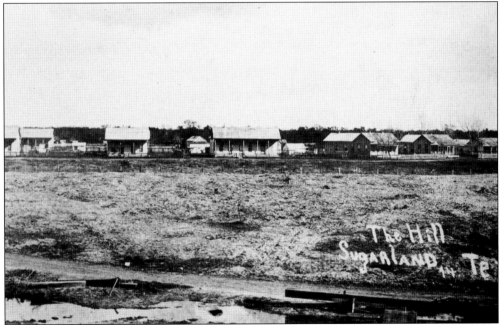

These 1890s houses on today's Second Street originally housed Cunningham's managers. They were built on The Hill, Sugar Land's first white neighborhood. It was the highest area in town and generally escaped heavy rains and frequent Brazos River floods. Over time, Kempner and Eldridge invested in dredging and water control measures to alleviate flooding.

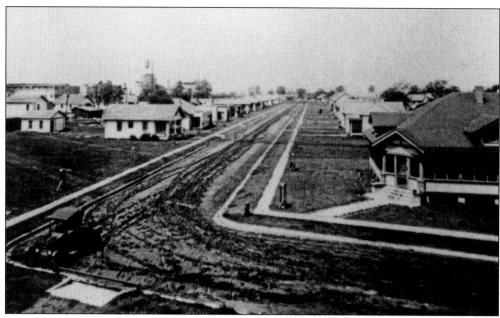

By the early 1920s, as lakes were dredged and low areas and swamps filled in, The Hill began to take shape. This picture of Second Street reflects the investment Kempner and Eldridge were willing to make to satisfy their workers. They built two- and three-bedroom frame houses with water, gas, electricity, and sewerage on curbed and guttered streets lined with sidewalks and newly planted trees.

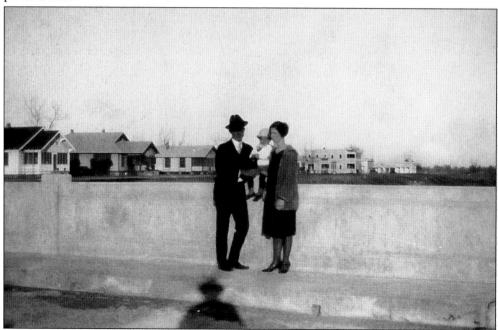

The Seitz family poses on the new Main Street Bridge in the 1920s. Some say The Hill got its name from an early footbridge at this location spanning Oyster Creek Bottom. The south bank was lower than the north, so pedestrians negotiated several steps on the north bank, mustering strength to meet the challenge. With a heavy load, it felt like encountering a hill, thus the name.

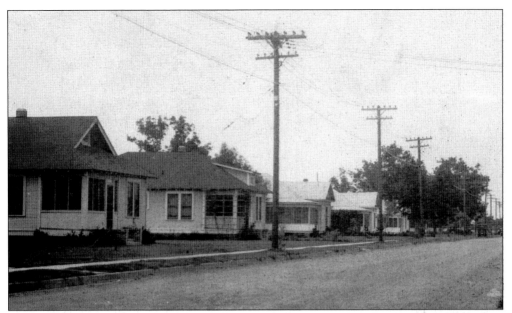

This early picture of Main Street on The Hill shows homes originally built for railroad workers. For the most part, houses were only for workers of Imperial Sugar, the Sugarland Industries, or the railroad; however, exceptions were made for some self-employed persons or employees of the few companies in Sugar Land not owned by Kempner or Eldridge, such as the Marshall Canning Company and Visco Products, Inc.

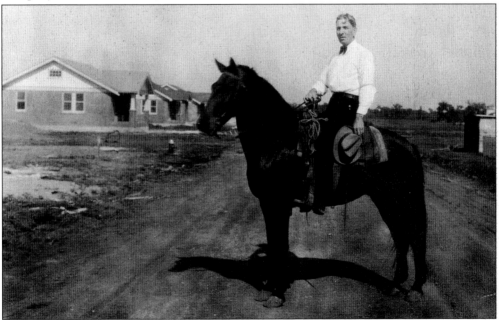

New brick homes are under construction in the background. The Hill has the greatest variety of architecture in old Sugar Land. Families took great pride in their rented houses, transforming barren, treeless yards into shaded, landscaped lawns and attractive gardens. The garden club planted watermelon-pink crepe myrtles along streets and beautified creek banks with plants and trees. Pictured is local resident A. L. Shields.

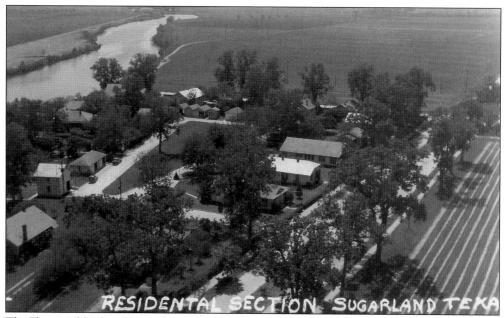

RESIDENTAL SECTION SUGARLAND TEXA

The Flats neighborhood located south of the refinery was originally built for management. Houses radiated from a courtyard accessible by car. At one time it boasted a tennis court. The company owned and immaculately maintained all the homes with crews of carpenters, painters, plumbers, electricians, and laborers.

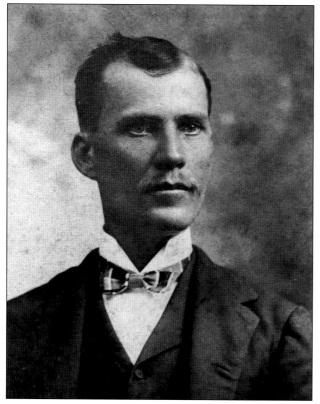

The Flats is bordered on the west by a street named for Capt. William McCan Brooks. Brooks Lake, surrounding local engineering firm Fluor-Daniel, also bears his name. He moved his family from their rural home on Brooks Lake to Brooks Street after being shot at through a window while handing his children a piece of sugarcane. Before becoming Sugarland Industries' farm labor boss, Brooks worked for the Texas State Penitentiary System.

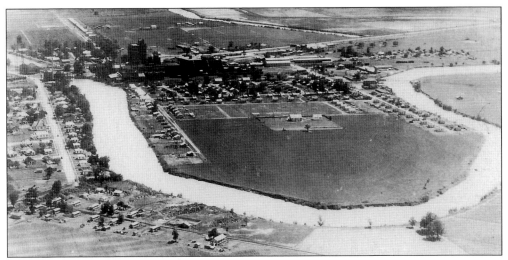

Not unlike other small Texas towns of the era, Sugar Land was racially segregated. North of the refinery, in the horseshoe bend of Oyster Creek, houses were built for blacks and Hispanics. Although livable, the homes did not have the amenities of the white neighborhoods, with limited water and electricity. In the 1950s, Imperial replaced them with solid-brick homes having all the modern conveniences.

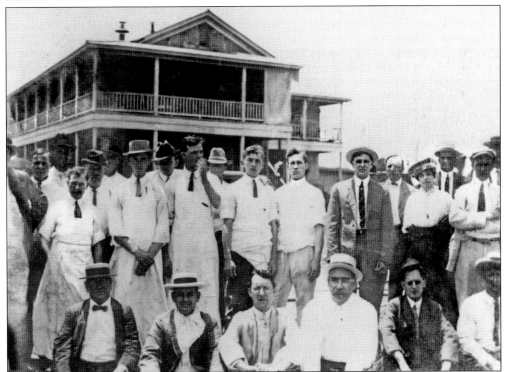

By 1913, a new stable workforce poses in front of the Attwood Hotel. Among those pictured are Hans and Willie Dierks who worked for their brother Charles in the grocery. M. R. Wood, Cunningham's chief chemist, recalled that, just a decade earlier, "the refinery operated only three months of the year and afforded (seasonal) employment to a small number of men—mostly drifters, besides the convicts."

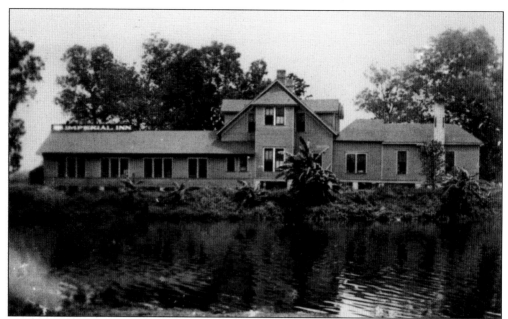

The Imperial Inn served as a hotel as well as a rooming house. It sat on the east side of Oyster Creek, just southeast of the refinery. Originally the old Thatcher Plantation house, it was moved from its Grand Central location (near the intersection today of Williams Trace and Lexington Boulevards) to become the Imperial Inn. It burned in 1947.

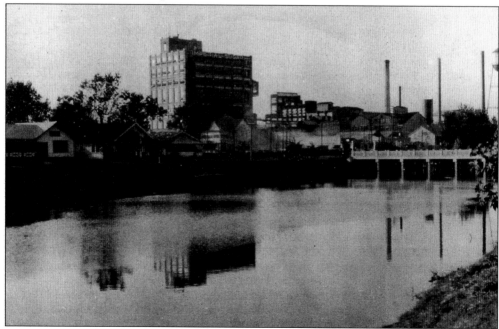

The first house on the left fronting Oyster Creek was Sugar Land's "teacherage," built in 1927 about a half a mile from the school. It was a safe place for single female teachers to live. The previous teacherage was too near the school for the teachers' liking, so they often rented rooms from local residents, leaving it unoccupied. Conveniently located next to Laura Eldridge Hospital, it was converted into a "nurserage."

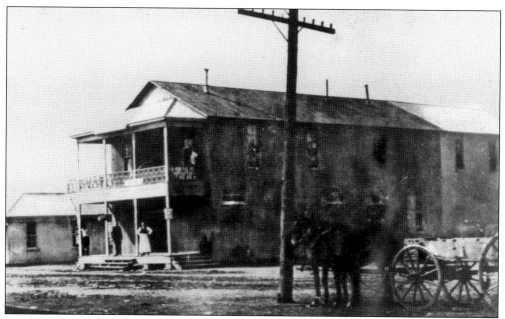

In 1908, Eldridge began cleaning up the commercial district, reusing the existing buildings—a pool hall, a commissary, and a couple of rooming houses. A lonely saloon keeper stands in front of his establishment in this early picture of Sugar Land's commercial district. The saloon would soon be converted to a produce and meat market.

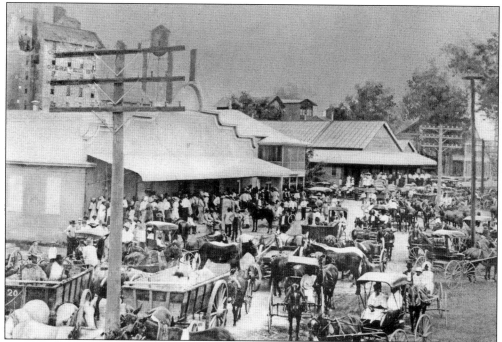

This 1913 photograph shows market day, when townspeople and farmers from the area gathered to shop and visit with friends and family who lived on other farms and had no time for visiting during the week. From left to right, the buildings in front of the refinery are the general store, drugstore, refinery office, and Eldridge home.

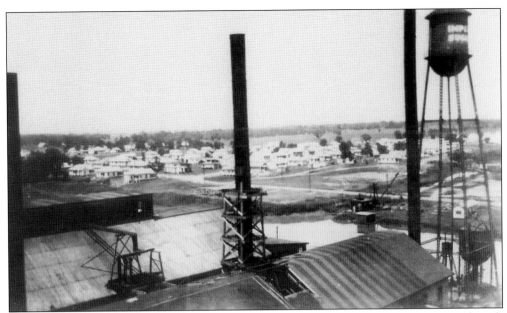

This late-1910s photograph shows The Hill before a canal would connect Oyster Creek with Cleveland Lake. The west end of First Street, still a swamp, would soon be transformed into a lovely row of bungalows.

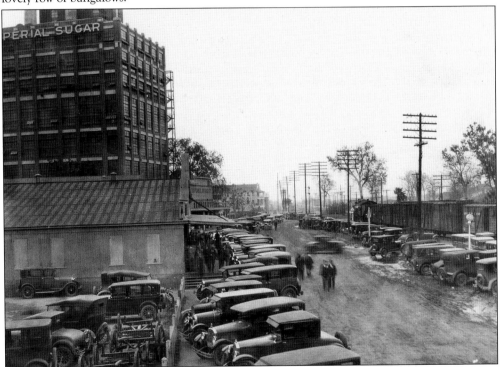

By 1925, Kempner and Eldridge had accomplished their goal to maintain and improve their industrial holdings while adding to and improving the infrastructure of the town. The newly constructed char house (left) stood as proof that they could build a viable business while creating a model company town that made workers proud.

Four

SUGARLAND INDUSTRIES

The Imperial Sugar Company owned and operated Sugar Land's enterprises, including the Cunningham refinery, until January 1, 1919, when the Kempner family and W. T. Eldridge organized a trust estate, Sugarland Industries, which would own and operate Sugar Land's various business activities—including Imperial Sugar.

Kempner and Eldridge appointed Gus D. Ulrich as general manager of Sugarland Industries. Ulrich had supervised the neighboring Sartartia Plantation for Eldridge since 1906, before being appointed to administer the partners' other Sugar Land interests, including the town and all enterprises as well as the surrounding 12,500 acres.

In 1924, the partners decided to expand the refinery and reformed the Imperial Sugar Company as a separate entity from Sugarland Industries.

Under the careful watch of Ulrich, along with Ike Kempner, and his son, Herbert, Sugarland Industries survived the 1930s Great Depression without a single job lost. Ulrich and his department heads kept close eyes on the financial and personal circumstances of every family to ensure help for those in need. Ulrich, known as "Mr. Sugar Land," managed almost everything in town until his death in 1947.

Fortunately, Herbert Kempner, Ike's son, had been involved in both Sugarland Industries and Imperial Sugar operations since Eldridge's death in 1932 and took Sugarland Industries' helm. By the late 1940s, Imperial needed more refinery workers. Instead of building more company houses, Herbert decided that the Sugarland Industries' Belknap Realty Company should offer lots to employees and non-employees alike. Private home ownership began in the Belknap and Alkire Lake subdivisions and along the south side of Lakeview Drive.

Herbert Kempner was responsible for improving town life in many ways. His untimely death in 1953 was deeply felt by Sugar Landers, who considered him one of their own and appreciated all that he had accomplished.

The well-respected Thomas L. James was then named president of Sugarland Industries. Starting as a stenographer for Ulrich in 1929, he eventually became the person in charge of gradually divesting the Kempner family of their Sugarland Industries holdings.

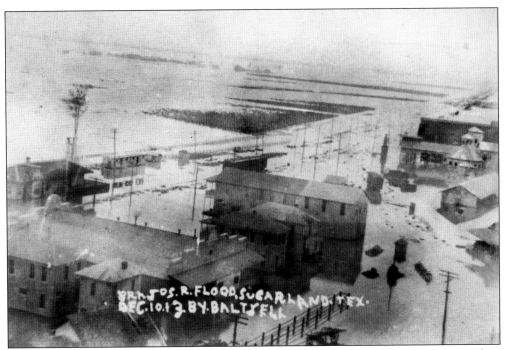

When Kempner and Eldridge took over Cunningham's Sugar Land property in 1908, it was low, swampy, and mosquito infested. Some called it the "Hell Hole of the Brazos." Frequent floods posed a serious problem. In 1913, heavy rains and water from the Brazos River covered the entire southern and western portion of the 7-mile-long plantation, right up to the door of the refinery.

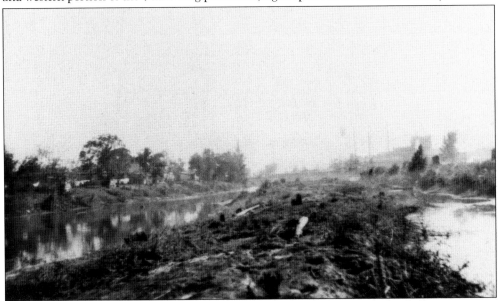

One of the owners' first acts was to dredge the swamps and streams and level the land. The shallow, swampy Oyster Creek, meandering past the refinery, was used for cooling water. It was often necessary to supplement it with water pumped from the Brazos River. Later another channel was dredged, connecting Cleveland Lake with Oyster Creek to ensure ample water for the refinery and neighboring agricultural fields, even during droughts.

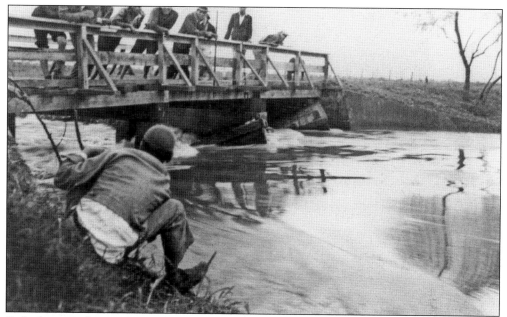

Onlookers watch as a torrent passes over one of three dams built to control Oyster Creek's flow. These dams and the Brazos River pumping station built during the Cunningham regime allowed Sugarland Industries officials to maintain the water in Oyster Creek and its tributary lakes at a reasonably constant level—within about 2 feet.

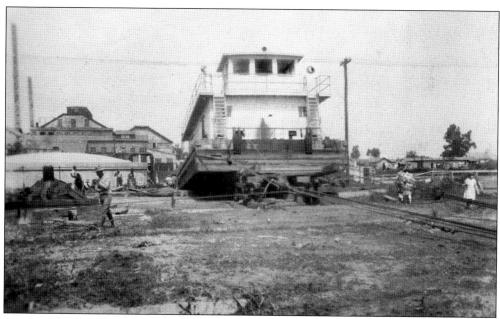

A crew is hauling a dredge boat overland from Oyster Creek to Cleveland Lake, where Main Street Bridge is today, around 1917. The dredge increased the lake's area to 40 acres at a maximum depth of 17 feet. After dredging the lake, workers cut a channel westward, connecting it to Oyster Creek, and used the earth to fill in a low area that is now First Street.

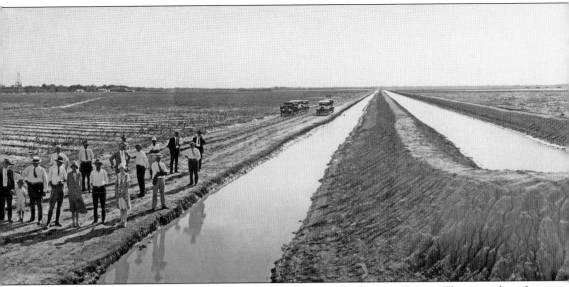

Sugarland Industries' 16-year flood control project included 8.5 miles of levees. They were from 2 to 14 feet high and 40 feet wide at the bottom. The project accelerated when heavy machinery replaced

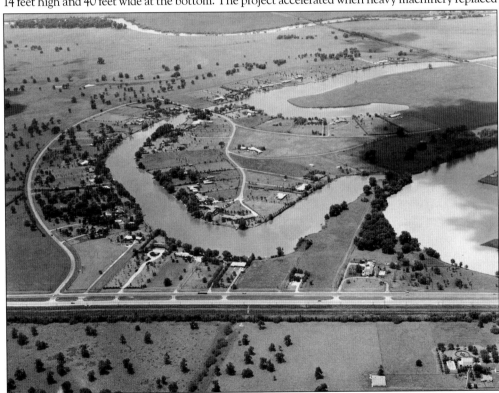

When the levees were completed in 1922, farmlands were leveled to fill in the ponds and swamps. Twenty miles of ditches drained the newly leveled land. The land could then be irrigated for growing farm crops along Oyster Creek. After World War II, Sugarland Industries began subdividing some of this land. This image shows roads and houses in the late 1940s surrounding Alkire Lake, once know as Alligator Lake. (Tom and Miriam James.)

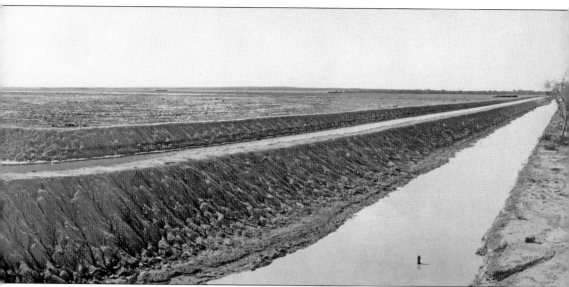

slow and laborious primitive tools. In 1921, representatives of the American Society of Chemical Engineers lauded Sugar Land's drainage and irrigation systems. (Tom and Miriam James.)

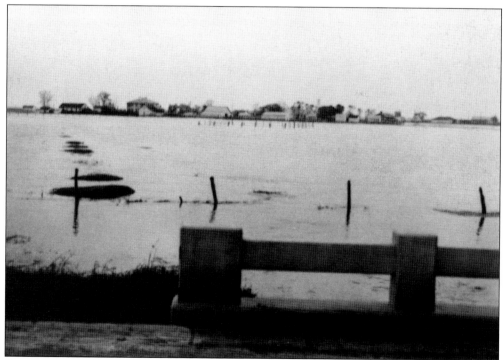

Heavy rains and Brazos River floods continued to occasionally inundate unprotected areas, such as the Texas State Penitentiary System's "Two Camp," now Telfair. Two-Camp and the surrounding acreage were outside of the Sugarland Industries' flood control project. Today authorities have taken additional water control measures to protect all of Sugar Land.

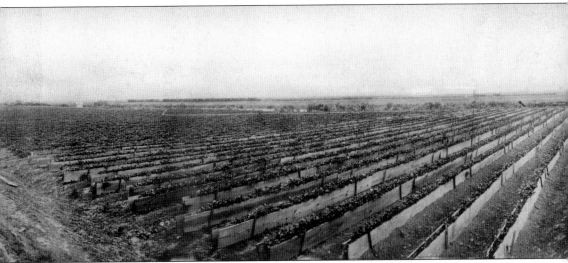

As lands were drained and filled in, acreage nearest the town became truck farms. Eldridge learned he could produce white celery by growing it aboveground in wooden troughs. He shipped his prized celery directly from Sugar Land in refrigerated railcars to waiting markets throughout

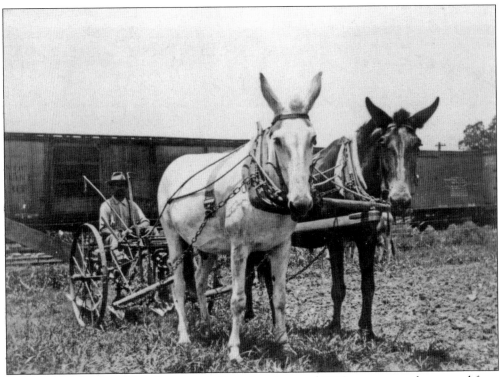

Tenant farmer Anton Pilz, who came to Sugar Land around 1916, operates mule-powered farm equipment for Sugarland Industries. Because reliable tenant farmers were hard to find, Sugarland Industries sent Pilz's son-in-law, Hans Dierks, to his native Germany to recruit farmers and their families to migrate to Sugar Land and work the land. Sugarland Industries offered a 50-50 share of the crop, a house, land, necessary machinery, and seed.

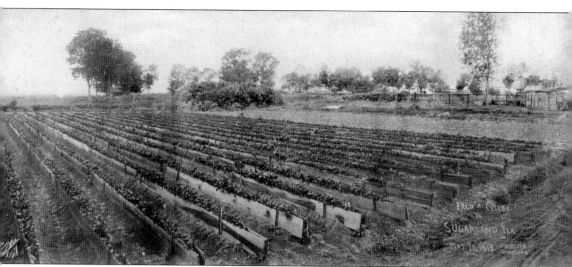

the country. Other crops included cabbage, spinach, mustard greens, potatoes, and citrus fruit. (Tom and Miriam James.)

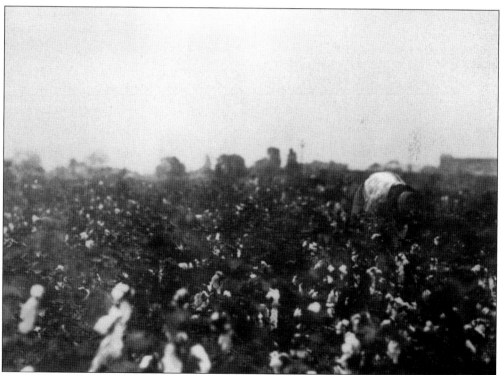

World War II depleted the labor force in and around Sugar Land, leaving Sugarland Industries heavily reliant on transient labor for harvesting. Sugarland Industries converted nearly half of its 11,000 acres to pastureland for herds of Hereford cattle. After the war, improved farm machinery helped solve the labor problem, and the land was again used for farming. (Fort Bend Museum Collection, University of North Texas.)

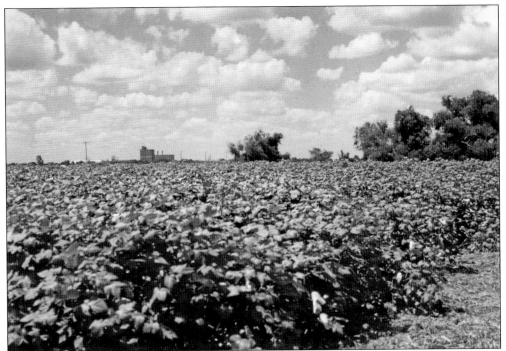

In 1927, Sugarland Industries grew 3,500 acres of cotton, yielding 2,500 bales. Its cotton gin did a booming business processing, baling, and selling the cotton to merchants, spinners, and shippers in Houston and Galveston. They also produced and sold registered cottonseed. The farms produced 101 bushels of corn per acre. (Tom and Miriam James.)

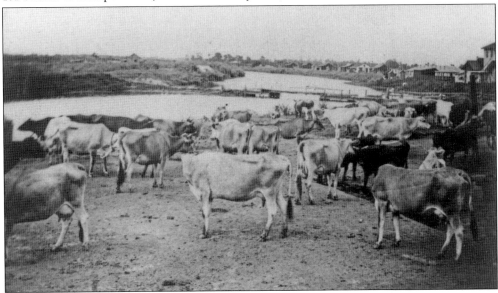

Dairy cows gather in the barnyard of the Imperial Dairy Farm. The dairy was located just west of the sugar refinery and north of Imperial Boulevard. A bridge connected it to a large outlying pasture within a large bend of Oyster Creek. The cows would find their way back and forth across the bridge each day to graze and be milked. The Imperial Mercantile sold the Imperial Dairy brand.

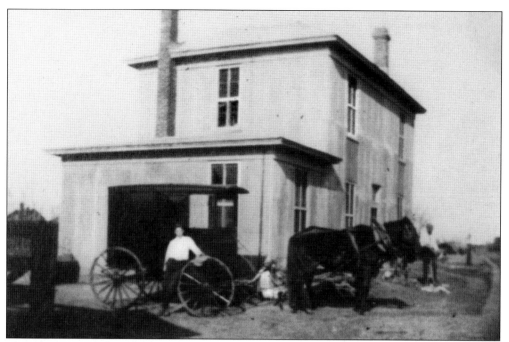

The dairy made daily home deliveries throughout Sugar Land. Other services also reached the homemaker's back door. Before the electric refrigerator, the iceman placed blocks of ice into iceboxes on back porches. A vendor sold fruits and vegetables door to door from a horse-drawn cart, and garbage was collected daily at the back door by a man driving a wagon with flowers laced in the mule's bridle. (Nan Scarborough Miller.)

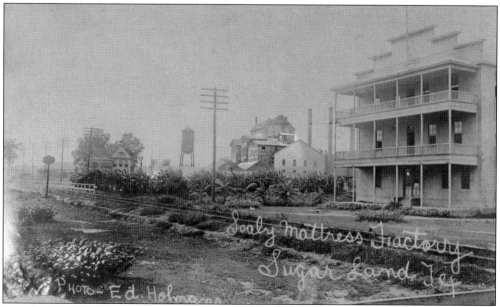

Sugarland Industries was the first owner of the Sealy Mattress trademark. They built a large three-story building in 1911 on the east bank of Oyster Creek for their new Sealy Mattress factory. With its home offices in Sugar Land, Sealy Mattress had plants located in Oklahoma City, St. Louis, Chicago, and Kansas City with a combined output of more than 500 mattresses per day.

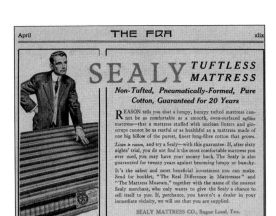

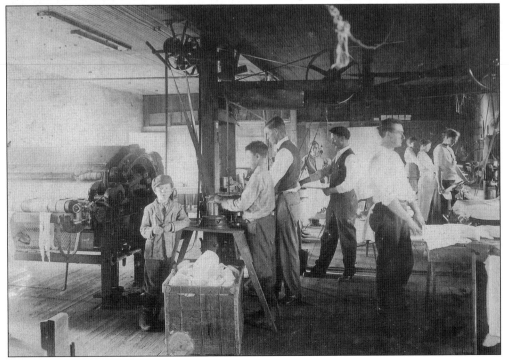

A young advertising executive, E. E. Edwards, launched Sealy Mattress on the road to national prominence by placing Sealy Mattress ads in publications such as the *Saturday Evening Post* and *Ladies' Home Journal* and penning the memorable Sealy slogan, *"Sleeping on a Sealy is like sleeping on a cloud."* Edwards bought the company and its trademark in 1925 and moved it to Houston. Below, workers are making Sealy "Tuftless" Mattresses in the Sugar Land factory. The building was later occupied by the Texas Fig Company, followed by the Marshall Canning Company. By the early 1920s, Sugar Land was fast becoming a small-town conglomerate boasting a meatpacking plant, acid plant, feed mill, poultry farm, furniture factory, railroad, and various retail outlets in addition to Imperial Sugar. (Bruce Kelly.)

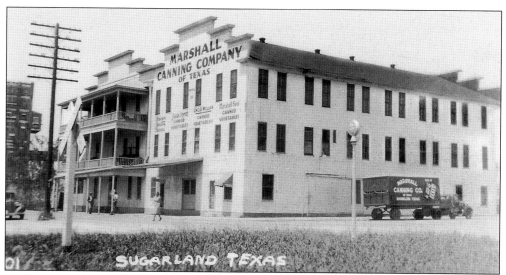

In 1936, Sugarland Industries persuaded Marshall Canning Company of Marshalltown, Iowa, to move to Sugar Land. Marshall contracted with farmers throughout Fort Bend to grow beans, cabbage, corn, sweet potatoes, spinach, and similar crops. With over 100 workers, the canning plant ran nearly around the clock, year-round, packing fresh vegetables in season and dried beans and peas in the offseason. (The Robert and Nona Laperouse family.)

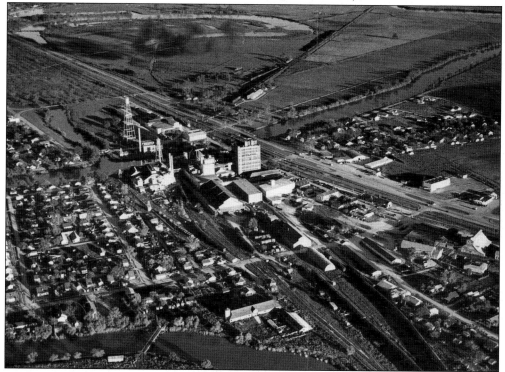

Eldridge designed Sugar Land to be worker-friendly. Most houses were within a block or two of the refinery and commercial district. This west-to-east view of early 1950s Sugar Land features Mayfield Park (lower left), The Hill (upper left), The Flats (upper right), Imperial Boulevard (lower right), and Imperial Sugar and commercial district (center). (Tom and Miriam James.)

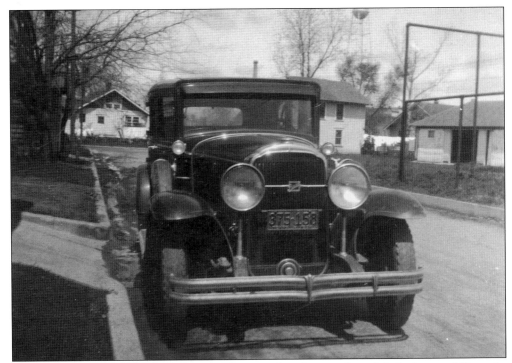

The Flats became home to many people who moved to the area from Schulenberg and Flatonia, Texas. Gus Ulrich, also a resident of The Flats, recruited storekeepers and craftsmen and built houses for them. Sugar Land soon became known as "Little Schulenberg" because so many of its citizens were of German and Czech descent. Hard-working people, the skilled workers built and maintained the houses, streets, sidewalks, and the water and sewage systems. (The Matlage family.)

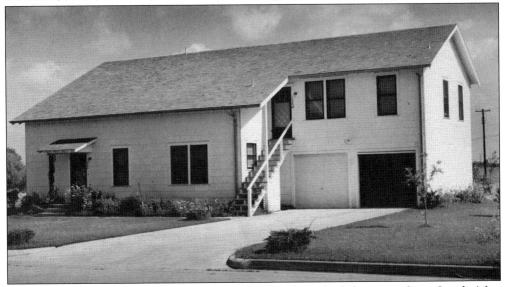

W. T. and Sallye Matlage built one of the earliest employee-built homes in Sugar Land. After World War II, Sugarland Industries sold lots to individuals to build their own houses instead of renting homes from the company. This small step toward individual home ownership eventually resulted in the incorporation of Sugar Land about 10 years later. (The Matlage family.)

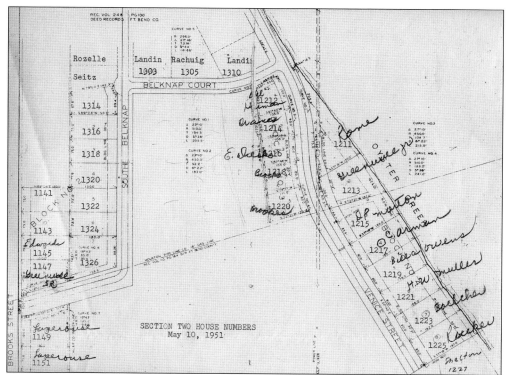

After World War II, Imperial had little difficulty attracting new employees to Sugar Land. Wages were comparable to Houston, work was steady, and the schools were excellent; it was a good place to live and raise a family. This 1951 map shows homes built in Belknap Subdivision, Section Two.

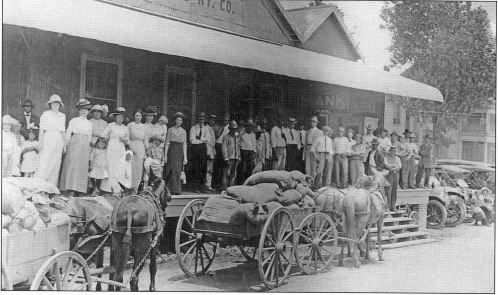

The Imperial State Bank occupied part of the general office building, which was constructed 4 feet aboveground to guard against floodwaters. It also housed the Imperial Sugar and Sugarland Industries office personnel, the post office, and the Western Union office. The mercantile and the various other retail establishments were along this block.

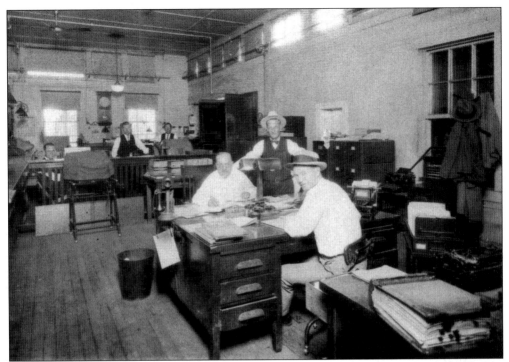

Imperial State Bank was renamed Imperial Bank and Trust. Its first statement of condition, dated November 1909, showed capital of $10,000, deposits of $20,589, and earnings of $258. This photograph depicts the bank interior when it occupied part of the company's executive office space. (Helmcamp Boatwright.)

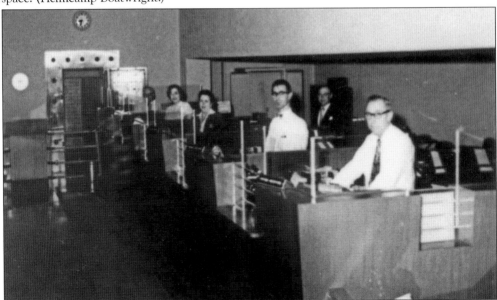

The new quarters of the Imperial Bank and Trust were located in the 1952 Sugar Land Shopping Center across U.S. Highway 90A from the sugar refinery. Pictured from left to right are Vic Krehmeier, Audrey Cooper, Mayme Rachuig, Ray Anhaiser, Boots Helmcamp, and Frank Usrey. The bank was renamed Sugar Land State Bank. (Helmcamp Boatwright.)

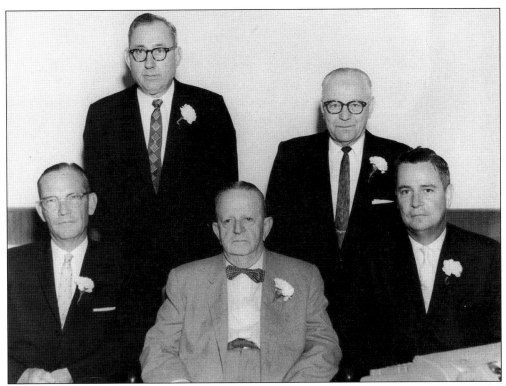

Imperial Bank and Trust received a new charter as the Sugar Land State Bank in 1955. The majority of the stock was sold to local businessmen and citizens of the community. Pictured from left to right are (first row) Thomas L. James, president; Lee Kempner, chairman; and Louis Merrigan, vice president/cashier; (second row) bank employees Frank Usrey and Vic Krehmeier. (Tom and Miriam James.)

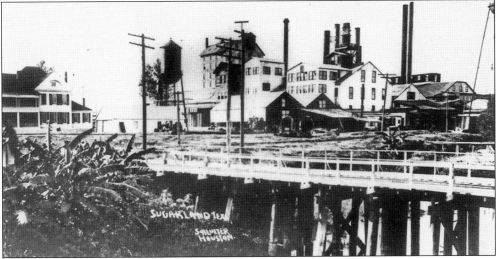

Good communication is essential to the success of any business. Sugar Land's telephone system originated in 1908 when partner and manager W. T. Eldridge had a phone line installed from his home to the plant superintendent in the refinery. During the town's early days, most business communications were conducted by mail, Western Union, or Postal Telegraph.

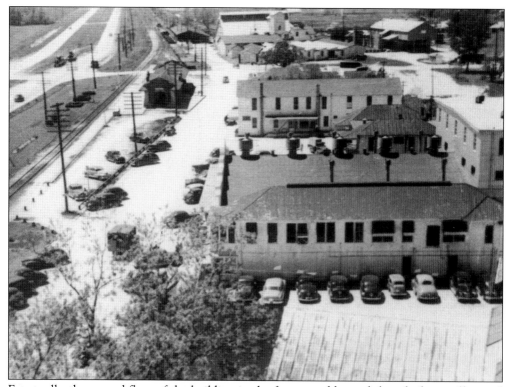

Eventually, the second floor of the building in the foreground housed the telephone office and switchboard, along with a doctor's office and beauty shop. Once installed, the phone system continued to expand, keeping pace with the growth of the town. The ground floor of the building housed a pharmaceutical shop and soda fountain, which included a popular feature, an ice cream machine.

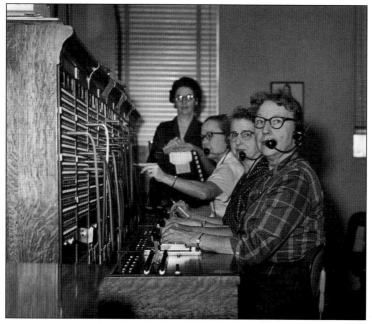

Switchboard operators answered, "Number, please." In the early 1920s, the phone system was limited; one person operated the switchboard per shift. When an operator completed a call to New York in a record-breaking four hours, Eldridge purportedly presented her with a box of candy. Pictured from left to right are 1950s operators Mildred Rozelle, Etna Schindler, Vela Rister, and Vic Kelly. (Charles Kelly.)

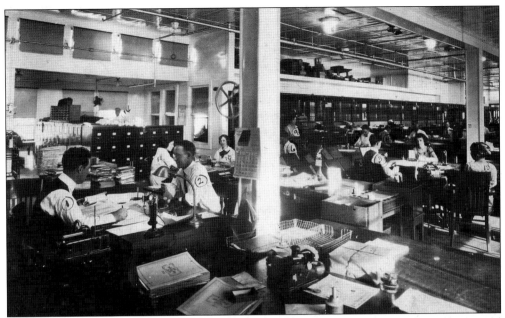

In the photograph above, employees go about their daily activities in the office pool of Imperial Sugar and Sugarland Industries in March 1921. This room served as Imperial Sugar's executive offices beginning in 1908. Sugarland Industries added their office operations there in 1919 after it was formed. The building was razed in 1952 when the executives and office workers of both companies found a new home across U.S. Highway 90A on the second floor of the new Sugar Land Shopping Center. In the early 1930s image below, office workers pose in front of the char house. (T. C. and Marjorie Rozelle.)

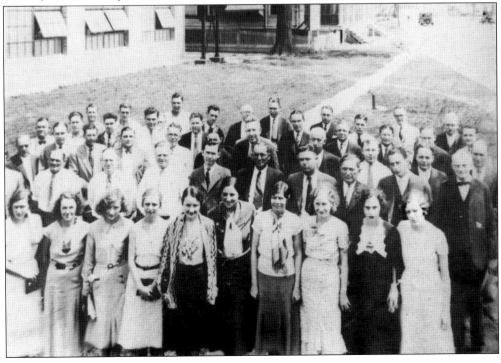

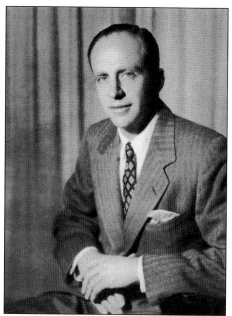

In the fall of 1945, Ike Kempner's son, Herbert, returned from the war to oversee reconstruction of the badly run-down refinery. He was vice president, treasurer, and a director of Imperial Sugar. Over $4 million was spent on plant improvements, with dramatic results. In 1949, both Imperial Sugar and the Sugarland Industries were operating profitably. The community mourned his untimely death in 1953. (Tom and Miriam James.)

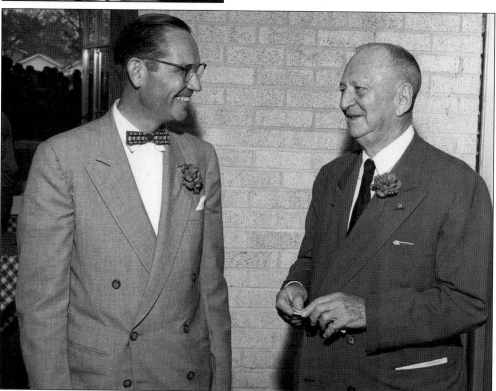

Following Herbert Kempner's death, Sugarland Industries was fortunate to have Thomas L. James. He came to Sugar Land in 1929 as Gus Ulrich's stenographer and worked his way up, becoming familiar with intimate details of the business. Ike Kempner (right) became Sugarland Industries board chairman, naming James (left) president. James would manage the complex of farms, real estate, and variegated small businesses for the next 26 years. (Tom and Miriam James.)

Five

SCHOOLS, CHURCHES, AND MEDICAL CARE

A community is enriched by the strength of its schools, faith institutions, and the quality of its medical care. Imperial Sugar ensured that its employees had the best available in all of these areas.

Education in colonial Texas was left to the individual. Dilue Rose Harris came to the area in 1833 at age eight and recorded the earliest-known account of a school in the Sugar Land area. She recalled the first teacher recruited as "an Irishman, old, ugly, and red-headed." He and her father canvassed the neighborhood and established a school for 12 students in an old windowless log blacksmith's shop. Supplies were scarce, books were borrowed from neighbors, and multiplication tables were written on donated pasteboard. Benjamin Franklin Terry hired a teacher to instruct his and neighboring children on his Oakland Plantation in 1853, but it was 1897 before the first school was built. The one-room school was replaced by a two-room school, and then in 1917 and 1918, the Sugar Land school campus was built, now called Lakeview Elementary. Its restored auditorium is currently Sugar Land's oldest public building.

In a small community, the school was often the meeting place for all significant gatherings. With no churches, the townspeople and various traveling preachers held services at the school's auditorium. In 1918, Imperial Sugar's founders donated four equal tracts comprising a single square block to four established local congregations. Land was also provided to the black community for a church. Each congregation met at the school auditorium on the corner of Wood and Second Streets until they were able to build. By 1927, each had a permanent building.

Medical care was scarce. The first known physician in the area was Dr. Pleasant W. Rose. He and his family landed on Galveston Island after a storm ran their ship aground. They traveled to Harrisburg via boat along Buffalo Bayou and, hearing of a farm for rent, traveled 20 miles west to Stafford's Point, settling in today's Quail Valley area. Decades later, the townspeople shared the services of a Texas prison doctor, but by 1920, Imperial Sugar built a hospital and made sure employees had the best medical care available.

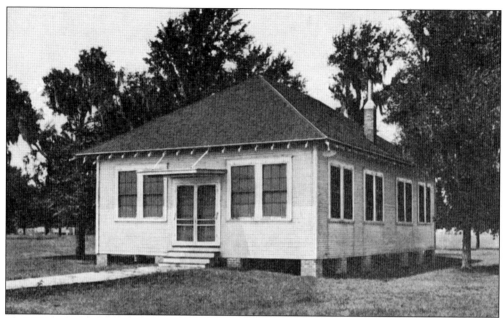

By 1897, one teacher taught in a one-room school at the corner of Second and Wood Streets (above). On weekends, the school served as a church facility. By the 1913–1914 school year, four teachers taught grades one through 10. Mary Anna Wood was principal and superintendent. In 1915, with Sugar Land's growing population, the one-room school was replaced with this two-room version below. Black children were taught in separate schools. By the late 1800s, there were three black schools in the area, including the Sugar Land Colored School, which opened in 1897. It was later renamed after Sugar Land's first school board president, M. R. Wood. Charlotte Mayfield served as principal from 1923 to 1944. The last segregated senior class graduated in 1965.

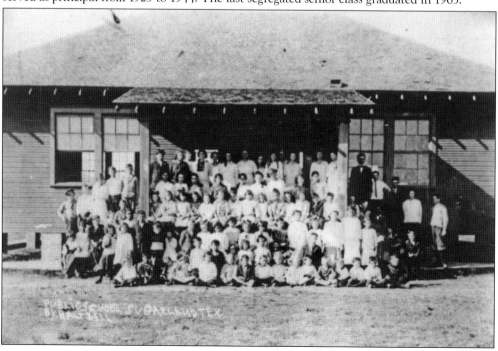

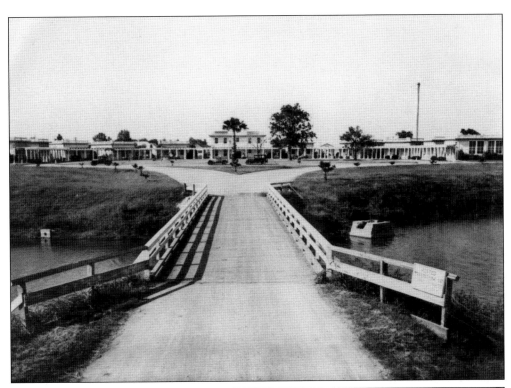

In 1916, W. T. Eldridge and Milton R. Wood traveled to California to observe the latest in school designs. Wood designed a school based on a Mission Revival–style campus they saw featuring an auditorium as the centerpiece of a state-of-the-art semicircular, 11-building school complex. Each cottage-style building housed different grades. Opened in 1917, the auditorium also became the community's social center, even hosting dances and events on its rooftop terrace.

Carrin Foreman was superintendent of the Sugar Land Independent School District (ISD) from 1924 to 1930. Her brother, famed trial attorney Percy Foreman, delivered commencement addresses in 1925 and 1928. Foreman left her position at Sugar Land to marry Fred Mauritz. She died March 1, 1932, while delivering her only child. (Woodson Research Center, Fondren Library, Rice University.)

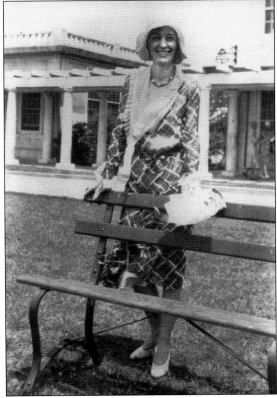

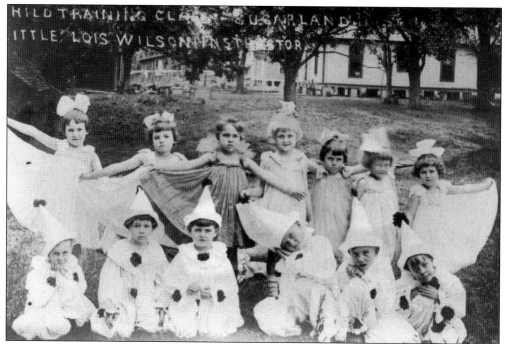

This c. 1920 photograph shows the first Sugar Land School kindergarten graduation exercise. Kempner's and Eldridge's commitment to a quality education was a testament to their philosophy of taking care of their workers' families. Rather than exploiting employees' children in their refinery and businesses, they sought to provide them an excellent education in a safe and pleasant environment. (Margery Brooks Ashford.)

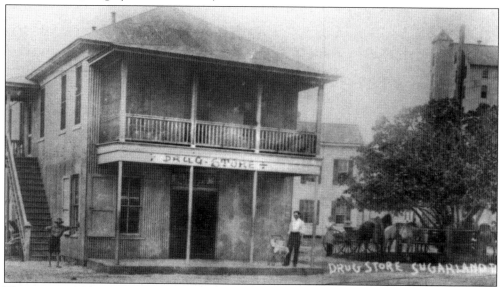

There were 400 houses in Sugar Land when Dr. Samuel Gayle Deatherage opened his medical practice above this drugstore in 1917. Seriously ill people were still treated in their homes or went to doctors in Houston or Richmond. Deatherage, originally brought to the area by the Texas State Penitentiary System as a prison doctor, was allowed to treat Sugar Land residents and eventually opened this office in Sugar Land.

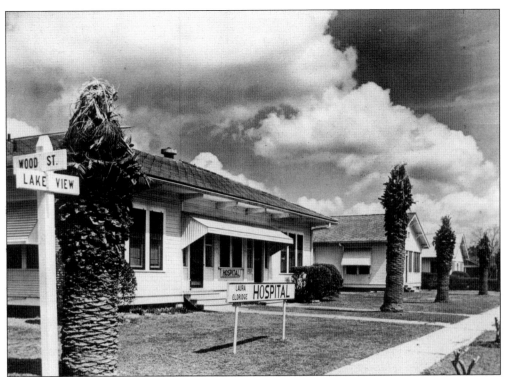

In 1920, officials decided to charter the first hospital in Fort Bend County. Three years later, Eldridge and Kempner invested $15,000 and built the Laura Eldridge Memorial Hospital. Doctors Samuel Deatherage, W. G. L. Blackwell, and later Carlos Slaughter, whose names were a local irony, provided quality care equal to that found in Houston. Imperial Sugar, the Sugarland Industries, and Sugar Land Railway provided employees full medical coverage for a fee of one percent of their monthly salary. In 1928, a young black man named Buster Brown was hired as a hospital orderly. The photograph below shows the hospital's two wings where residents of all races received separate but excellent medical treatment in connected facilities.

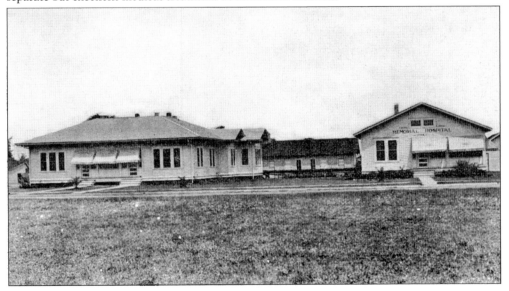

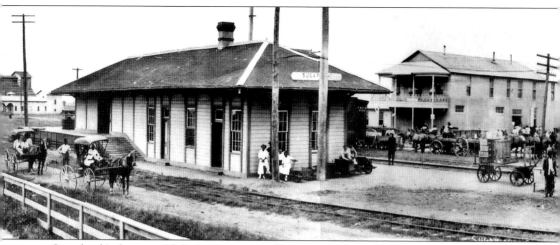

Sugarland Industries and the Sugar Land Railway provided endowments ($165,000 in cash and land valued at $10,000) for hospital construction and ongoing employee benefits. Employees received benefits including complete medical and surgical treatment, outpatient services at the doctor's

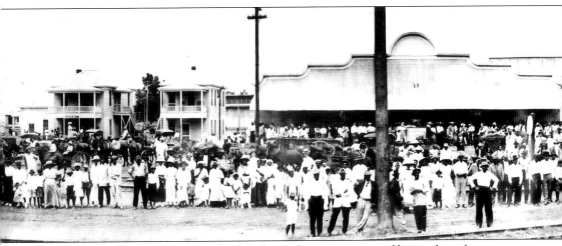

office, all medication, eyeglasses, artificial limbs, and up to one year of hospital confinement. Workers' families were treated at modest cost as well.

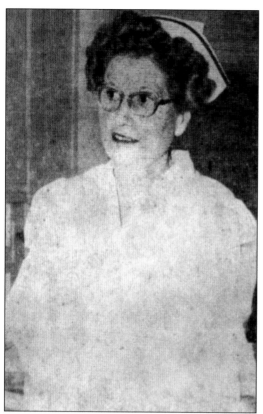

Nema Sheppard, R.N., who was affectionately known to patients and staff as "Miss Nema," joined the hospital on January 13, 1932; she later became its superintendent. She managed the establishment—including the doctors—with a velvet hand to the general benefit of the entire community. Sheppard retired on October 19, 1964, after serving Laura Eldridge and Eldridge Memorial Hospitals for 41 years.

In 1956, the hospital relocated to the east side of Eldridge Road on land donated by Imperial Sugar and the Kempner family interests. The $358,000 facility was built and funded with endowments from Sugarland Industries and the Missouri Pacific Railroad. The hospital had the best physical plant and equipment available at the time and was an important benefaction to the community. (T. C. and Marjorie Rozelle.)

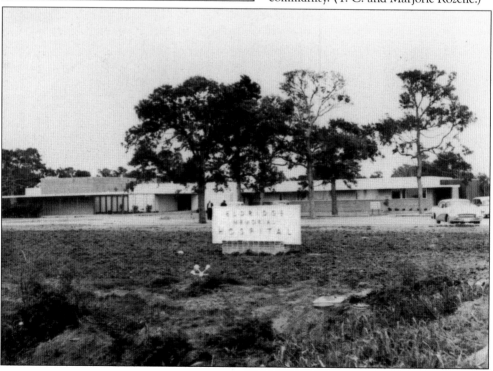

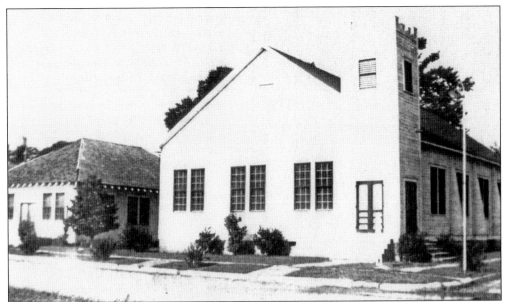

On September 14, 1914, Rev. G. H. Williams organized an 11-member church with monthly services. In 1919, the church purchased a school building and moved it to the southwest corner of Fifth and Wood Streets. A new sanctuary was built in 1939, and the old building was used for education. The congregation changed its name to First Baptist Church of Sugar Land in 1949.

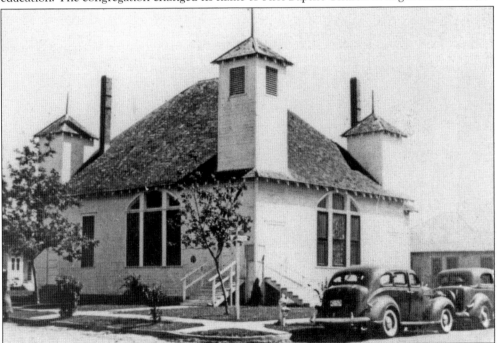

A Methodist congregation was formed in 1912. Operated on a tight budget, they disbanded, reorganized, and fell apart again. The church was reorganized for a third time in 1919 and has continued since. A wooden structure (pictured) at Main and Fourth Streets served the church until 1956, when the congregation bought three acres of land on Eldridge Road for a new building. (Robert and Nona Laperouse.)

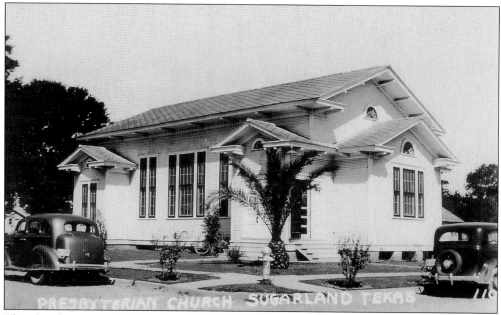

This church was organized October 6, 1916, as a 14-member home mission of the Brazos Presbytery. First Presbyterian Church (pictured) was later constructed at the northwest corner of Fourth and Wood Streets. The congregation voted to sell this property in 1960 to the Baptist congregation, who built on the corner of Fifth and Wood. The new church building at 502 Eldridge Road was occupied by this congregation in February 1962. (Robert and Nona Laperouse.)

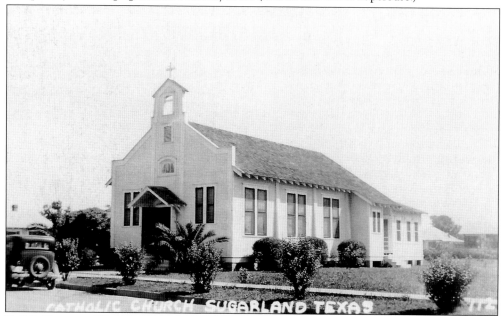

Fr. I. P. Tonson, of Houston, held Mass every fifth Sunday beginning in 1916 at the home of Jessie H. Roberts on Main Street. Mass was later held at the school at Wood and Second Streets before moving to the Sugar Land school auditorium in 1918. A wooden structure (pictured) with a bell tower was constructed in 1925 at Fifth and Main Streets. St. Theresa's was named a parish in 1935. (Robert and Nona Laperouse.)

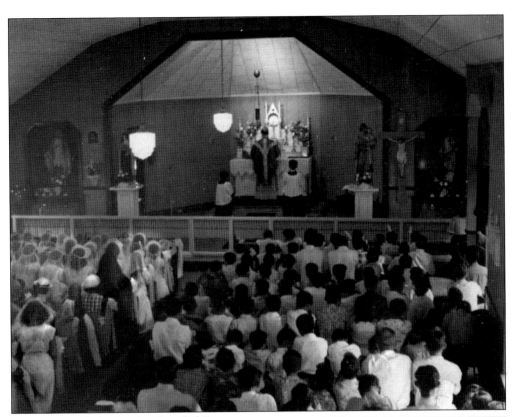

The city's Catholic families founded St. Theresa's Catholic Church in 1918 after Imperial Sugar gave them land at the corner of Fifth and Main Streets to build the wood-frame building seen in these photographs. Pictured here is a First Communion service held in 1946. Immediately after this service, Lupe Rodriguez Cavazos (left) and Margie Ramirez proudly posed just outside the sanctuary's front doors in their First Communion attire with St. Theresa nuns Sr. Rose Marie (left) and Sr. Elizabeth. St. Theresa's current facility is now located two blocks from its original site at the corner of Seventh and Main Streets. (Lupe Cavazos.)

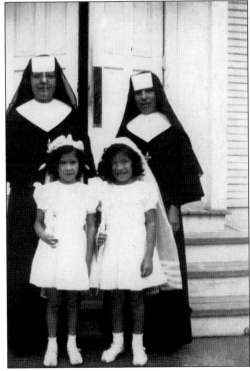

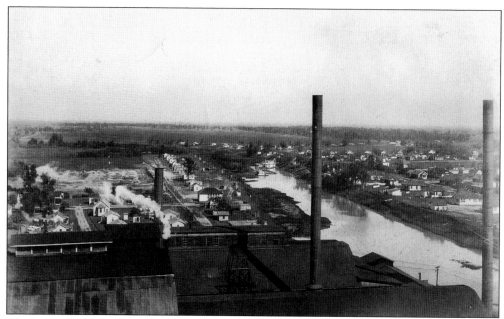

The largest building above in The Quarters was a social hall (center), which was also used as a church meeting hall. Black residents remained outside the original four congregations and established two Baptist churches, Pleasant Spring and Mount Calvary. In 1954, church leaders agreed to merge congregations and build one place of worship. On June 12, 1955, the first worship service was held at Mount Pleasant Missionary Baptist Church, led by its first pastor, Rev. R. L. Robinson, who served from 1954 to 1960. Pictured below in the forefront in front of the church is Rev. Eddie Thomas, who has served as the church's pastor since September 1961. (Below, Curley and Agnes Thomas.)

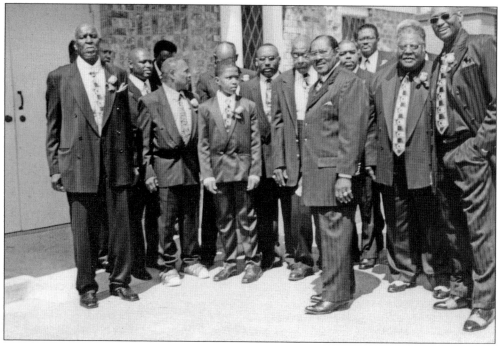

Six

LIFE IN A COMPANY TOWN

Sugar Land was a quiet, isolated little town on the Texas coastal plain. Most Sugar Landers found diversion from their day-to-day routine within the community. They took infrequent trips into Houston or traveled farther afield on their yearly vacations, but their principal amusements were close at hand.

The townspeople found a wealth of experiences and opportunities to occupy their free time, when they were not working or raising their families. Sports activities were, of course, important in the small Texas town. Imperial Sugar sponsored amateur baseball and softball teams for years. Central to community life and town identity, the school produced championship football teams in 1938 and later in the early 1950s. The Sugar Land Gators and running back Ken Hall still hold many national high school football records.

The 1918 school complex served as the social center of the community. Silent movies, traveling entertainment, and educational programs were held in the auditorium, and dances and other social activities were held on its tiled rooftop terrace.

In the early 1950s, the Palms Theater opened its doors, providing four decades of movie entertainment. Later in the decade, the Lions Club and St. Theresa's Catholic Church sponsored two Little League teams.

Before the school's heated pool opened in the early 1930s, youngsters congregated at any one of the towns lakes to swim and picnic. After the school pool became obsolete, the Lions Club and the Kempner Foundation built a community pool that is now the first of many serving the city.

Quality of life in Sugar Land was rich. Mothers looked after each other's children in the tightly knit community. Everyone had a job, and crime was minimal. Even during the Great Depression, no one was laid off from work. Although racial segregation persisted through the 1960s, town life was relatively harmonious.

Even the transition from company-owned town to incorporated city was accomplished with minimal disruption. Many families have stayed in this rural industrial town for generations, watching it grow into a vibrant, thriving, diverse city.

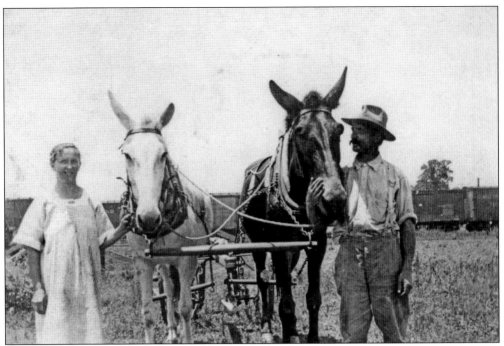

Ana Schraber and Anton Pilz (pictured) emigrated from Austria to Texas in 1913. Three years later, they moved to Sugar Land to farm part of the vast acreage owned by the Sugarland Industries. Even though motorized farm equipment was available, most of the farm equipment was animal-powered. As late as World War II, their daughter Elsie delivered Imperial Dairy products by a horse-drawn wagon. (Elsie Dierks.)

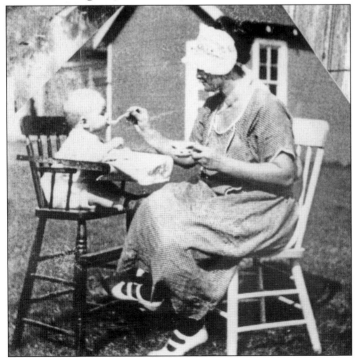

Sybil Fowler delivered the first baby born in Laura Eldridge Memorial Hospital in December 1923. Providing a built environment for families began in earnest around 1916, and the young Fowler family proved that workers and their dependents were finding Sugar Land a good place to live. Fowler later became Sugar Land's first serious historian, laying the foundation for subsequent researchers. (Muffet Guenther Gideon.)

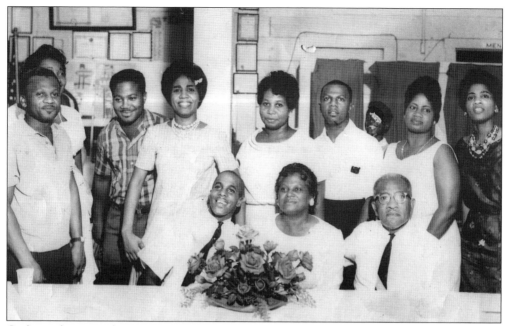

Curley and Agnes Thomas's family met in 1963 for a family reunion. Curley and Agnes are seen here with their children, from left to right, (first row) Ernest, Agnes, and Curley; (second row) Sterling, M. C., Mildred, Bobbie, Charles, Eunice, and Thelma. Rosie and Frank are absent. (Curley Thomas.)

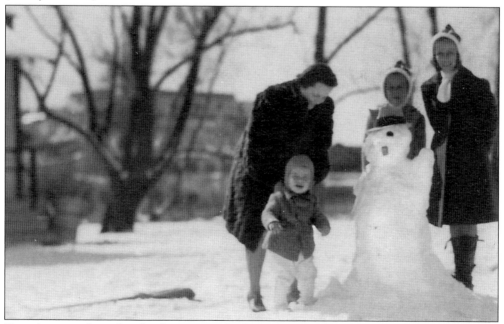

Over the years, Sugar Landers have enjoyed infrequent snowfalls in spite of the area's subtropical climate. The Laperouses sculpted a snowman around 1940 in the front yard of their house fronting Oyster Creek in The Flats. Mother Nona supports her toddler, Robert Allen, as older sisters Gloria (behind snowman) and Wynell stand with pride over their creation. (Robert and Nona Laperouse.)

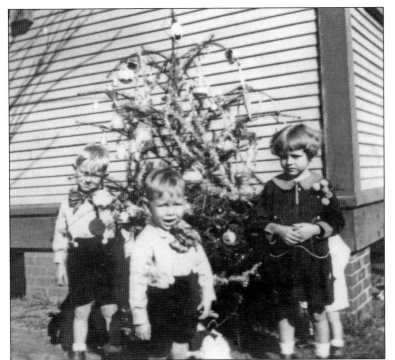

Sugar Land children benefited from the handsome cottages and bungalows with big yards. Homes featured electric lights, water, and indoor bathroom facilities not often afforded to workers in company towns. From left to right are Fred, Charles Anton, and Dora Marie Dierks by their house where Frost Bank stands today. (Elsie Dierks.)

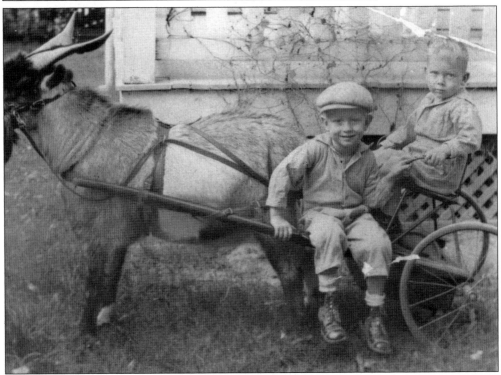

The Dierks brothers, Fred (left) and Charles, ride in a traveling photographer's goat cart. After the boys' father died, their mother hired on as a refinery worker. Company officials hired deceased employees' widows and work-aged children so families could remain in their homes. (Elsie Dierks.)

This young equestrian, Leon Anhaiser, was born and raised in Sugar Land and attended local schools. Anhaiser won a Kempner scholarship and attended LSU; he received a Sugar Engineering degree in 1961. He became Imperial Sugar's refinery plant manager and vice president of refinery operations. (Leon Anhaiser)

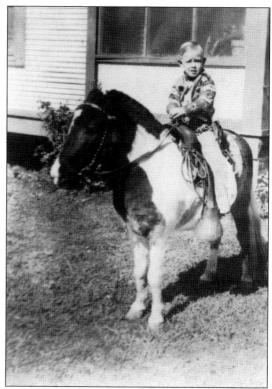

In January 1952, young Sugar Landers enjoy ice cream at the grand opening celebration of the new Sugar Land Shopping Center, across U.S. Highway 90A from the refinery. The shopping center replaced the metal-clad buildings of the old commercial district in front of the refinery, about where the new sugar silos now stand. The old drugstore was razed, but the Imperial Mercantile survived, becoming the Sugar Land Farm and Home Center. (The Reyes III family.)

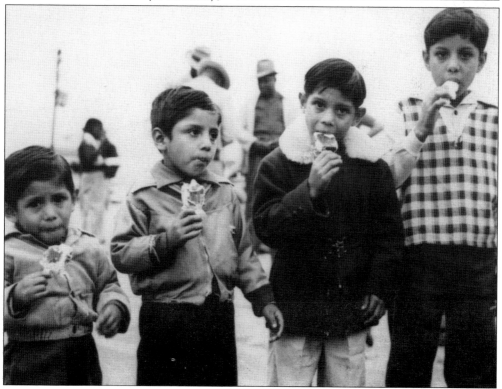

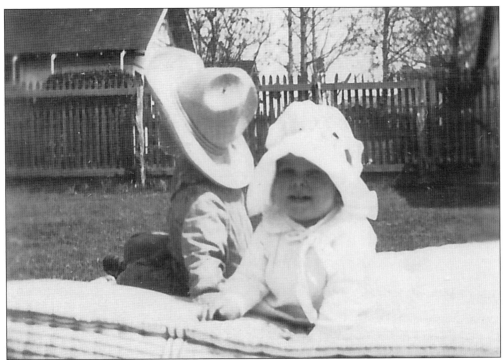

Although there were three major neighborhoods, The Hill, The Flats, and The Quarters (later named Mayfield Park), another one existed along Imperial Boulevard, just west of the refinery. Toddlers Rennie (left) and Betty Pirtle bask in the sun, perhaps on a Sealy Tuftless Mattress made in Sugar Land. Locals jokingly called Imperial Boulevard "Rat Row" after rodents feeding on seeds and grains stored nearby. (Jess and Martha Pirtle.)

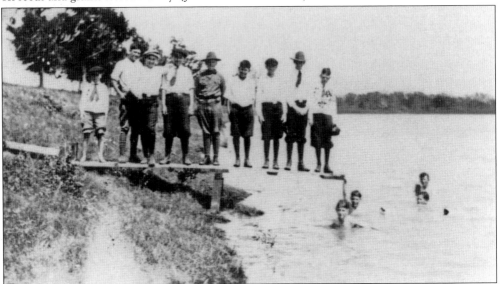

Before the days of air-conditioning, swimming was a popular way for youngsters to cool off in Sugar Land's sultry summers. Water control measures taken from 1917 through 1930 provided an ample number of small recreational lakes. Even after officials built a heated indoor swimming pool at the school in 1931, many youngsters still preferred the outdoor swimming hole. (A. G. Starr.)

Ida Seitz and Leroy Urban emphasize the size of a monster catfish caught in Oyster Creek. Many of the company houses backed up to or fronted the creek. Despite an occasional alligator or water moccasin, families could swim, boat, and fish from their yards. Many youngsters learned to bird and rabbit hunt on the vast acreage surrounding the town. (Ida Seitz-Pokluda.)

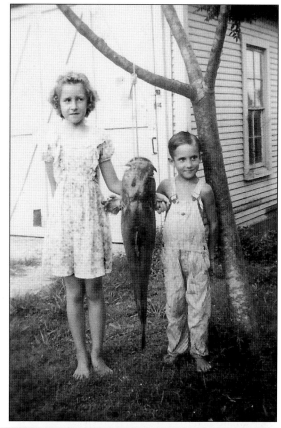

Before desegregation, the Texas Central Prison Unit at Sugar Land had separate facilities for whites and blacks. The unit for blacks south of U.S. Highway 90A was known as "Two Camp," and the unit for whites north of the highway was "One Camp." (Texas Department of Criminal Justice.)

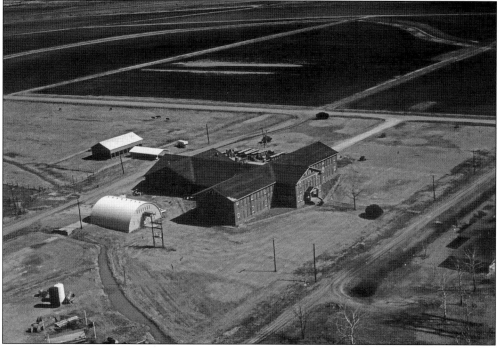

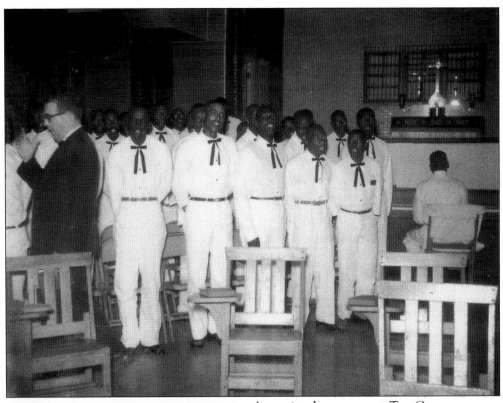

A convict chorus poses at Two Camp, probably a routine part of religious services sponsored by the prison. A less organized but more popular type of music transcended prison walls throughout the South—the blues. The origin of "Midnight Special" is sometimes incorrectly attributed to this prison; one version does, however, warn the listener to walk right or be Sugar Land bound. (Texas Department of Criminal Justice.)

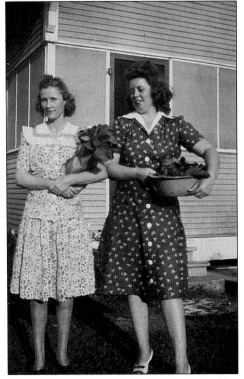

Humble Camp residents Verdie Ehrlich (left) and Mayme Rachuig display produce from their World War II Victory Gardens. Humble Oil maintained an oil field, pipeline pump station, and a small refinery on Sugarland Industries' property, about 5 miles southeast of Sugar Land, from the 1920s through the 1950s. Sugarland Industries operated a store there, and Humble built a swimming pool, recreation hall, and playground for their workers. (Mayme Rachuig Hause.)

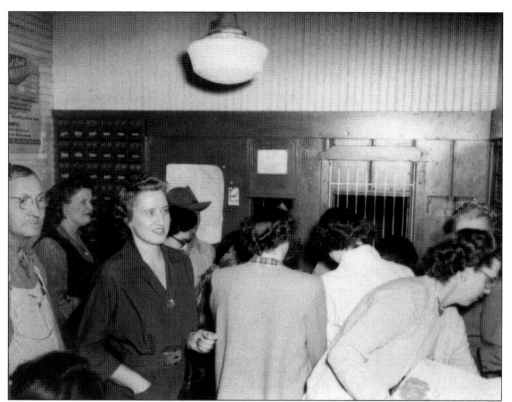

It was not until the mid-1950s that Sugar Land was big enough to have home mail delivery. Up until that time, one of the daily social interactions of the townspeople took place at the post office. It was here they would often exchange local news and gossip in the tiny postal facility located in the front of Imperial Sugar's executive office building next to the char house. (Robert and Nona Laperouse.)

Apart from nursing and teaching, women generally did not hold positions of authority in Sugar Land. Nina Mae Iiams, however, broke the glass ceiling. She was known to exercise her power as postmistress, strictly following the official postal regulations to the occasional confusion and frustration of local patrons. (Robert and Nona Laperouse.)

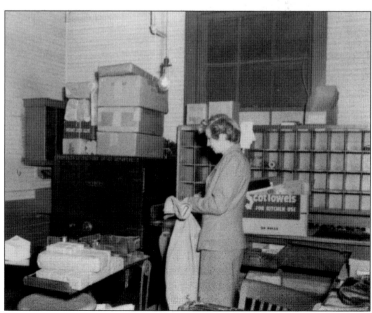

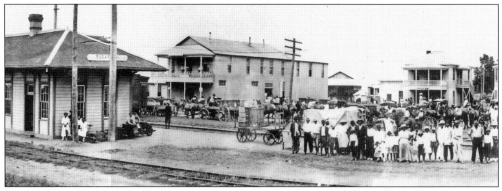

The two-story building in the center provided ample opportunities for men to spend free time in the sleepy small town. In 1908, when Eldridge began managing the town, it was used as a saloon and pool hall; he soon converted it into a respectable meat and produce market. The Fraternal Order of Odd Fellows met on its second floor in the 1920s, later the Congress of Industrial Organizations (CIO) Union.

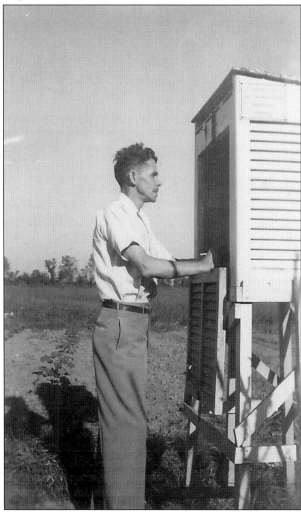

Bob Laperouse was a multitalented man. He officially monitored Sugar Land weather (pictured), took excellent photographs, and played the piano and organ. He began as a sugar chemist and retired as vice president of refinery operations. Other men enjoyed hobbies such as stamp collecting, gardening, and woodworking. When tired of being alone, some men would gather for cigars, adult beverages, and a friendly game of poker. (Robert and Nona Laperouse.)

A former teacher, Jess Pirtle came to Sugar Land with his family in 1924. They lived on Main Street but moved to Imperial Boulevard a short time later when new houses became available. He started out working on the construction of Sugar Land's tall water tower and was the silent movie projectionist in Sugar Land's school auditorium. Pirtle eventually retired as the official engineer and surveyor for Sugarland Industries. (Jess and Martha Pirtle.)

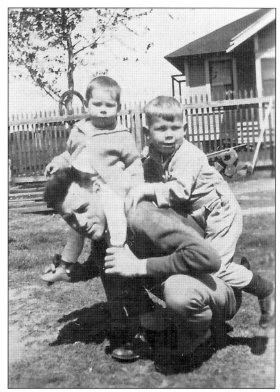

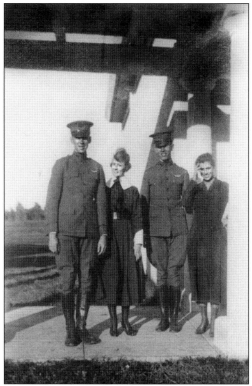

Two doughboys and their young lady friends visit under the columned pergola at the brand new Sugar Land School. The only Sugar Lander who lost his life in World War I was Lonnie Green. A park bordered by Main, Fourth, Fifth, and Wood Streets was named in his honor. To make room for additional company houses, the park was relocated to a strip of land between First Street and Cleveland Lake. (Alice Phelps Storm.)

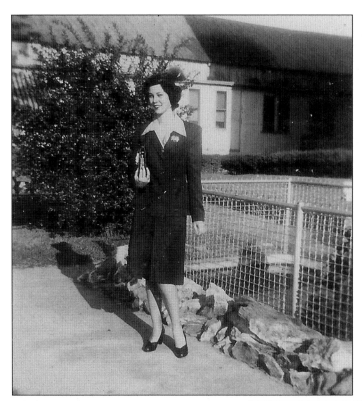

Bound for college, Betty Pirtle McClure stands by the koi pond in front of the char house around 1940. Young people of Sugar Land benefited greatly from their parents' employment in Sugar Land. The Kempner family emphasized quality education for their workers' children. Not only did they build a unique, state-of-the-art campus, they also hired excellent administrators and teachers. A large percentage of Sugar Land High School graduates attended college. (Jess and Martha Pirtle.)

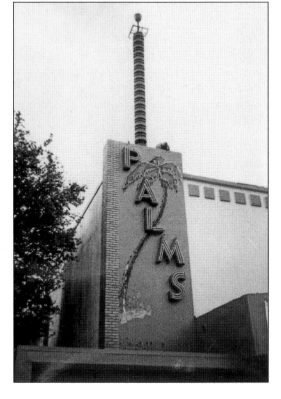

To the delight of the townspeople, the Palms Theater opened in 1950 on the southeast corner of Ulrich Street and U.S. Highway 90A. The theater's South Seas theme complemented the palm trees lining Highway 90A. The auditorium resembled the deck of a ship, and the walls above were painted with murals of small islands, palm trees, and clouds, giving one the sense of floating in the middle of an ocean. (Helmcamp Boatwright.)

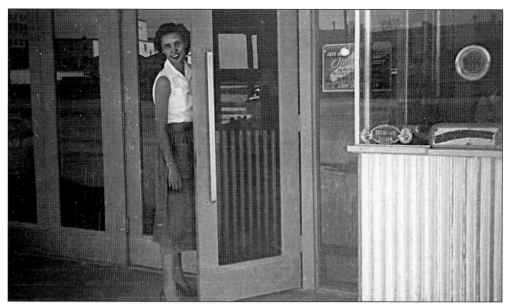

In the early 1950s, employee Mickey Wanjura stands at the entrance to the Palms Theater, where Sugar Land's famous Kenneth Hall, who still holds U.S. records in high school track and football, was a ticket taker and usher. Minorities sat in the upper balcony or could attend the monthly movie "tent shows" in The Quarters for 7¢. (Ida Seitz-Pokluda.)

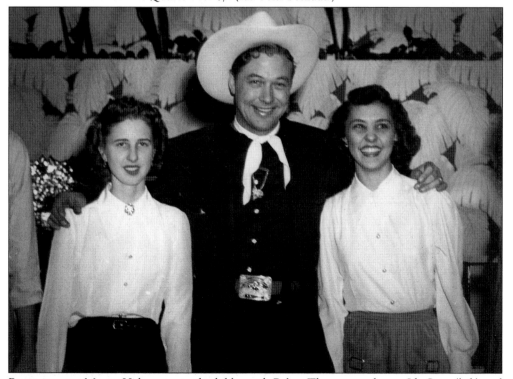

B-movie actor Monty Hale poses in the lobby with Palms Theater employees Ida Seitz (left) and Mickey Wanjura. The theater had a stage for magic and specialty shows. Hale died in 2009. (Ida Seitz-Pokluda.)

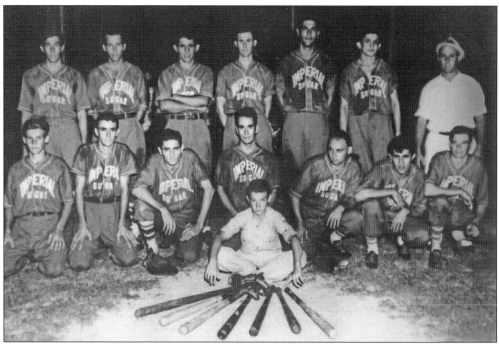

Baseball and softball were major pastimes for the town. Imperial Sugar sponsored softball and baseball teams for many years. This photograph shows the company's 1938 softball team. From left to right, they are (first row) batboy Tootie Douglas; (second row) Ralph McCord, Otto Hrncir, Bill Harman, Monroe Elskes, Sparky Brock, Walter Prikryl, and Vernon Hill; (third row) Carter Lomax, Carroll Scarborough, Rudy Pagel, Leroy Starr, J. W. Boston, Leo Pagel, and coach Frank Schultz. (T. C. and Marjorie Rozelle.)

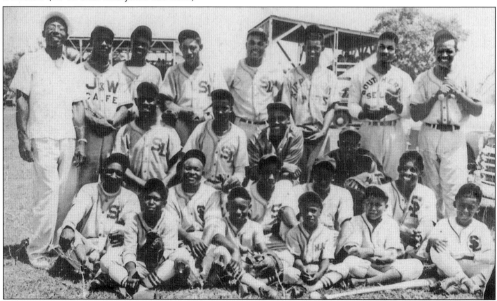

The all-black team, the Tigers, also sponsored by Imperial Sugar, played in a field north of Nalco. Before games Leon Blackburn would advertise the event through a megaphone atop his car, notifying local residents when a game was about to begin. (D. C. Pickett.)

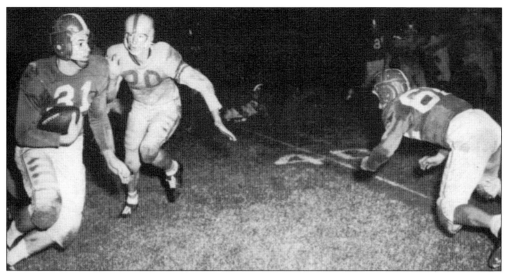

Kenneth Hall, Sugar Land's celebrated running back, races through an opponent for a long gain. Many of Hall's high school career records are unsurpassed to this day. He ran 11,232 yards and averaged 32.9 points per game. These records are even more astounding because Hall rarely played in the second half or even past the first quarter. He changed into his band uniform and marched, playing trumpet at halftime. (Sugar Land ISD.)

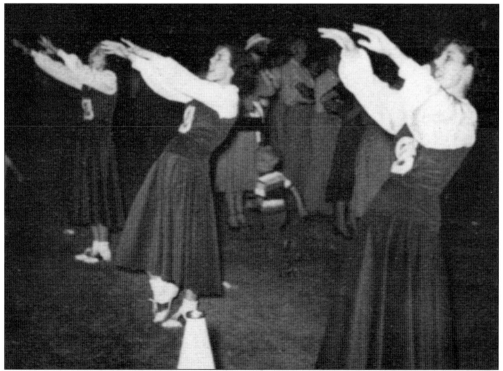

From left to right, Evelyn Garnoski, Eloise Coburn, and Jo Anderson lead cheers at a 1953 Sugar Land Gators football game. Virtually all residents watched the Gators on their phenomenal winning streak. One old-timer recollects that Imperial Sugar employees working in the refinery on Friday nights would call the press box at Kempner Field for updates on the game. (Sugar Land ISD.)

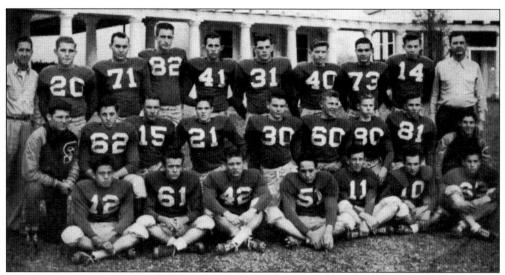

The Gator teams of the 1950s had a rare combination of speed and agility, as demonstrated by the fact that they won the Class B Texas State Track and Field Championships in 1952 and 1953. The 1953 Regional Champions pose for their team picture on the Sugar Land High School campus, which is the present location of Lakeview Elementary School. (Sugar Land ISD.)

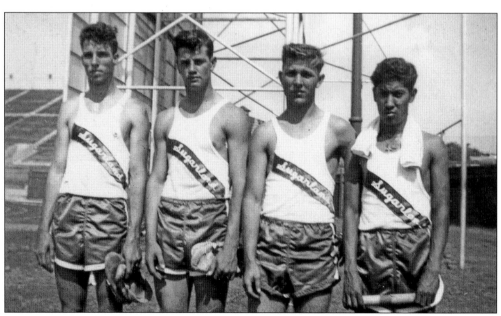

Teammates (from left to right) George Salmon, Kenneth Hall, J. B. Kachinski, and Earnest Trevino stand in the south end zone of Memorial Stadium in Austin during the 1952 Texas State Track Meet. They won first place in the 440-yard relay race. (Ernest Trevino.)

Athletic success was not confined to men's sports. Sugar Land High School's girls' basketball teams of the late 1950s were a raging success, going to the Texas State Tournament in 1958. Georgia Binford and Melva Kelton were all-state selections. Georgia Binford won the Babe Zaharias Award as an outstanding female amateur athlete in 1958. In this photograph, Sugar Land High School is playing Santa Fe High School. The three Sugar Land girls in the back are, from left to right, Babs Bissett, B. J. Binford, and Janet Kruger (behind shooter). Georgia Binford and Melva Kelton are not pictured. The girl on the left and the shooter are unidentified players from Santa Fe. (Sugar Land ISD.)

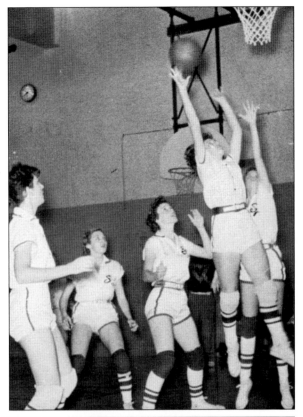

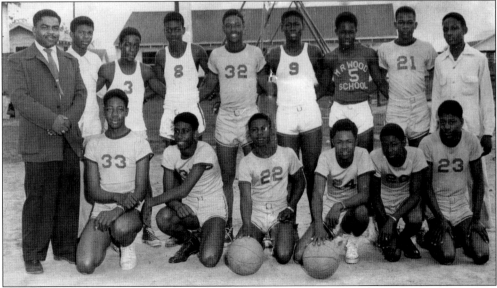

The M. R. Wood basketball team poses for a picture in the 1950s. Although Sugar Land schools were segregated through the mid-1960s, the M. R. Woods School was highly successful in athletic competition. The football team, led by coach Hollis Felder with the assistance of Leon Mooring, led the M. R. Wood Panthers in a phenomenal winning streak of eight consecutive district football championships in the 1950s and 1960s. (Curley and Agnes Thomas.)

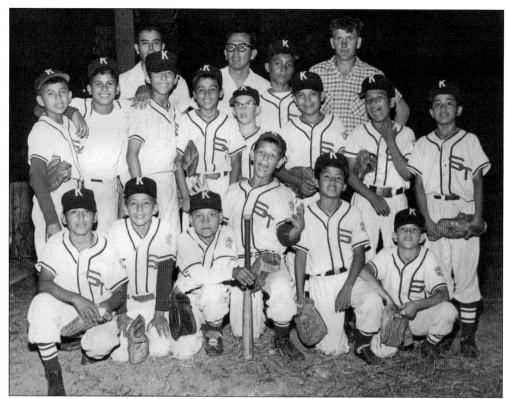

In 1963, the St. Theresa Knights won 30 consecutive games. From left to right, they are (first row) Joe Martinez, Roland Rodriguez Jr., Alfred de la O, Johnny Pena, Eddie Mendoza, and Fred Hamlin; (second row) Joe Morales, Ronnie Rivera, Richard Rangel, Carlos Moreno, John Hamlin, Albert de la O, Richard Mendoza, Valente Rodriguez, and Alex Flores; (third row) coaches Arthur Ramirez, Roland Rodriguez, and Ray Allen. (Julia Moreno.)

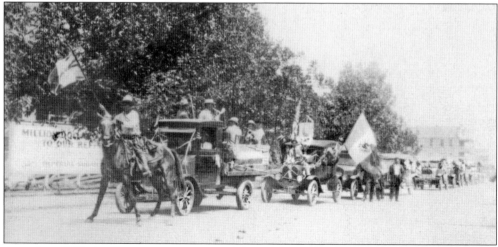

As early as 1925, the Hispanic community celebrated Cinco de Mayo along Sugar Land Street in front of the refinery. The date commemorates Mexico's victory over French troops in the Battle of Puebla on May 5, 1862. In the United States, the holiday takes on a different significance by celebrating Mexican culture and the Hispanic American experience. (Tom and Miriam James.)

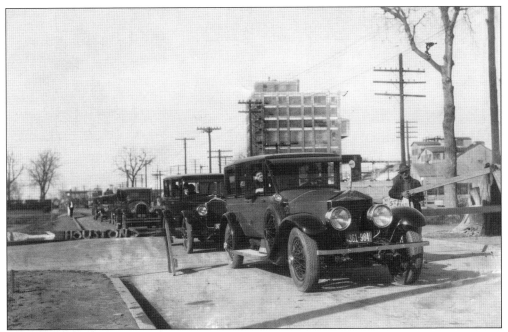

In 1927, front-seat passenger W. T. Eldridge rides in the first automobile to drive eastward toward Houston from Sugar Land on the new cement-paved highway. It replaced the gravel and oyster shell road subject to potholes and washouts. (Tom and Miriam James.)

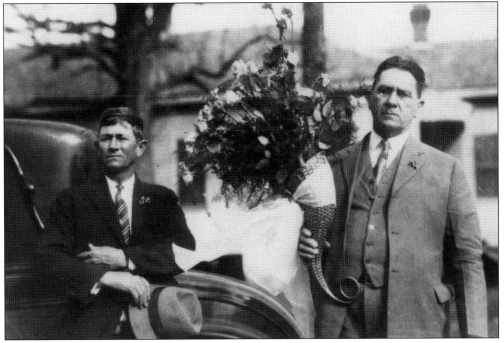

County commissioner I. G. Wirtz (left) attends a funeral around 1930. Sugar Land did not possess an undertaker or funeral parlor. Some families had their viewings at home, with funerals held at one of the local churches. The Hispanic community had the San Isidro cemetery at Grand Central, but non-Hispanics buried their dead elsewhere in the area. (T. C. and Marjorie Rozelle.)

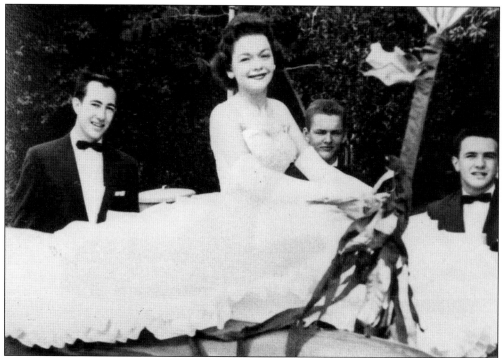

Sugar Landers enjoyed participating in county-wide events. In the mid-1950s, Fort Bend County Fair Queen contestant Jonellen Wheeler participates in the Fort Bend County Fair Parade with her escorts, (from left to right) Ray Barton, Tommy Cason, and Frankie Rogers. Fort Bend County schools and municipalities supported and participated in the annual fair parade, usually held at the end of September in Rosenberg and Richmond. (Sugar Land ISD.)

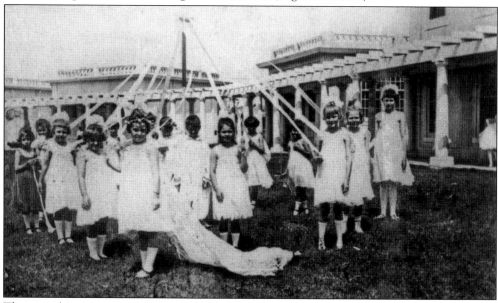

The annual Spring Festival, begun with the 1918 opening of the cottage-style school, was renamed the Sugar Festival during which King and Queen Ragus (sugar spelled backward) attended court, with neighboring schools invited to the event. (Elsie Dierks.)

Seven

CITY INCORPORATION

During the 1950s, with the City of Houston annexing everything in sight, Ike Kempner went on the offensive with annexation plans for his company town. At that time, Imperial Sugar operated everything in town. The acreage consisted of both Imperial Sugar and Sugarland Industries. An interesting historical note is that the lawyer who drew up the charter for Sugarland Industries mistakenly spelled "Sugar Land" as one word. It was never changed, and city leaders work hard to this day to ensure others spell it correctly as two.

To ramp up for incorporation beginning in 1957, company houses were sold to the employees living in them, creating homeowners who could vote to become a general law city. An election was held on December 29, 1959, and five aldermen and the city's first mayor, T. E. Harman, held Sugar Land's first city council meeting on January 19, 1960. The newly incorporated city spanned 4 square miles with a population of approximately 2,500. Throughout the 1960s, the company transitioned services to the new city government. The city hired its first city employee—city secretary Hazel McJunkin—and scheduled council meetings on the first and third Tuesdays of each month, a practice that continues today.

City growth was slow, but important early decisions laid the groundwork for future success. The creation of a comprehensive plan paved the way for zoning. The plan was the first of many that charted an orderly, planned, and systematic development of the city. The document built on the business plan of the company town's founders, Ike Kempner and W. T. Eldridge.

An important step during the 1960s was the creation of a city police force. Sugar Land hired Joe Burke to the newly created position of city marshal. When the city assumed responsibility for the water and sewer system, a third employee was hired.

Those early hires laid the groundwork for Sugar Land's current workforce of 641 employees; they provide comprehensive services for the city's population of 79,573.

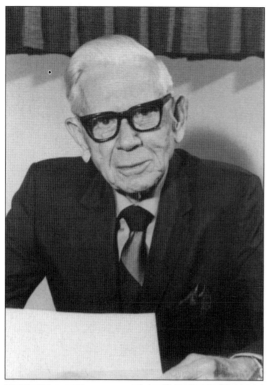

On December 15, 1959, T. E. Harman was elected the first mayor of Sugar Land to serve with five aldermen; the six were officially sworn into office on December 29. When he assumed office, the brand-new city had no staff, no equipment, no permanent home, and no money.

On the cold and rainy day of December 15, 1959, over 70 percent of the registered voters, 480 citizens, turned out to elect the city's first mayor and five aldermen. Pictured from left to right are Melvin Pomikal, alderman; Bill Little, alderman; Minnie Ulrich, alderwoman; Fort Bend County Judge Clyde Kennelly; Mayor Ted Harman; Jess Pirtle, alderman; and C. E. McFadden, alderman. Sugar Land was now officially a general law city, with a population of about 2,000.

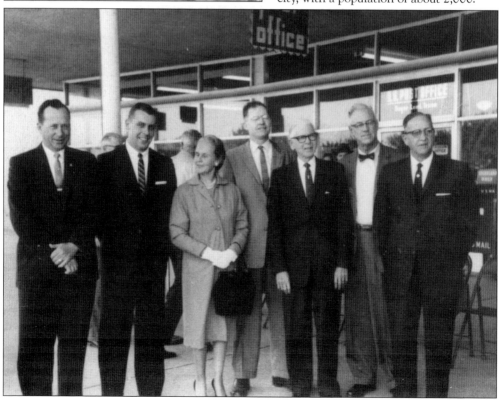

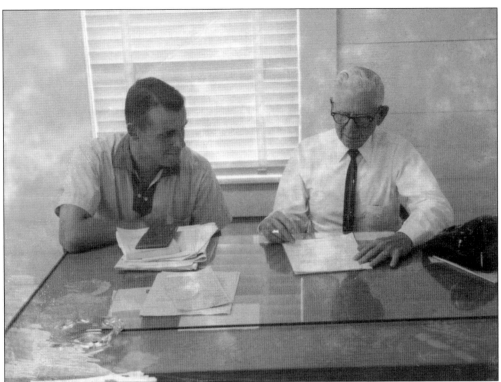

Following incorporation, the Sugar Land City Council asked Imperial Sugar for a building to turn into city hall. The company provided a shoe store on Kempner Street that included one office and an additional room. The sugar company donated desks and chairs, and the local Lion's Club provided additional furniture for the council table. Councilman Bill Little is pictured with the mayor.

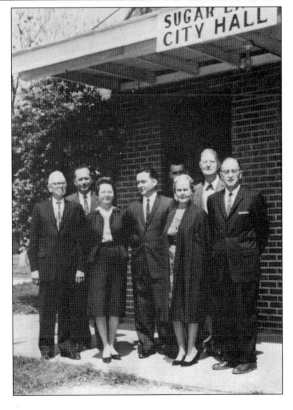

The first Sugar Land City Council meeting was held on January 19, 1960. The city received its first bill, an invoice for $200 from its attorney. The bill was approved with payment deferred. As the city grew and became financially stronger, land was purchased on Brooks Street for the second city hall. (T. C. and Marjorie Rozelle.)

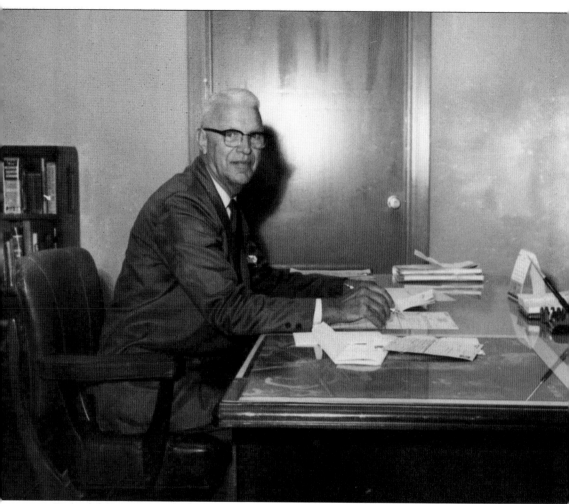

One of the city council's first actions after incorporation was to approve building, plumbing, and electricity codes. This was followed by the implementation of a comprehensive city plan in 1961, which allowed for the incorporation of zoning. Pictured is Sugar Land's first city building official, Albert H. Weth.

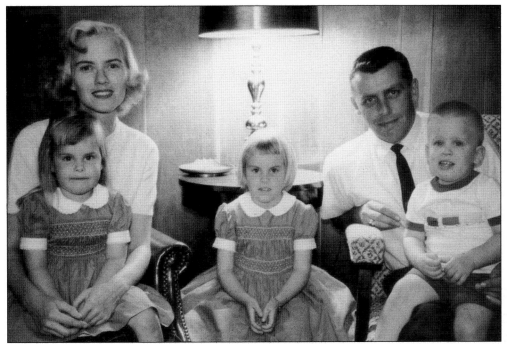

Bill Little was elected mayor in 1961, just a few years after the city's incorporation. He and his wife, Mary, came from Ohio looking for job opportunities in Sugar Land, and he found one with Sugarland Industries. During those days, there were not many new people in the company town, but they would have a lasting impact on the city's future.

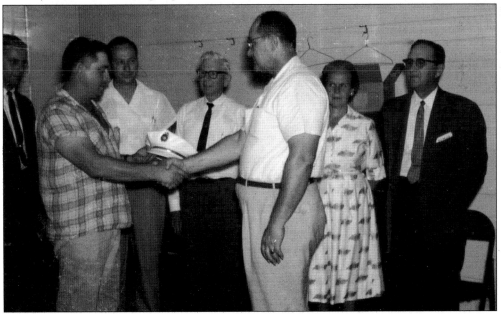

The City of Sugar Land's first fire chief was Walter "Soapy" Borowski. Volunteer firefighters listened for the refinery steam whistle. It would sound a set number of blasts to indicate which part of town was experiencing a fire. A ring-down telephone later served the purpose of today's 911, ringing in many of the members' homes and at Imperial Sugar.

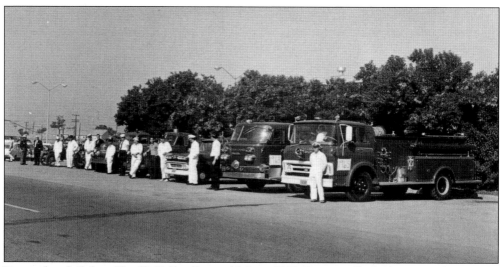

Pictured with Police Chief J. E. Fendley and Mayor T. E. Harman (far left) are members of the Sugar Land Volunteer Fire Department. Volunteers, most employed by Imperial Sugar, provided fire protection in Sugar Land after incorporation. The change to a full-time career department occurred in 1978 with the hiring of Arnold Finch, Sugar Land's first paid professional firefighter, who is now retired.

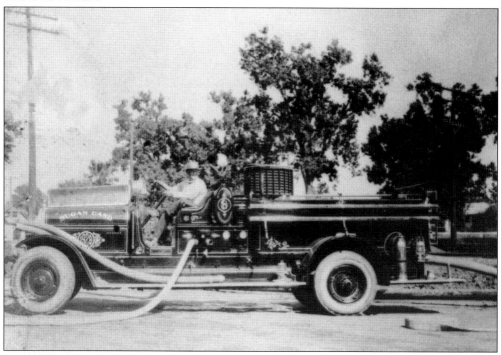

Fire marshal Gerald Cullar recalled, "My father worked across from the fire station. I watched the firefighters responding to calls and training with the old 1927 Seagraves and 1947 Chevy fire engines. I learned the old steam whistle codes, which identified where the fire was located. I would go and watch. I began to volunteer in 1976, while working for Imperial Sugar. We responded from the plant in a Chevy panel truck." Pictured driving the Seagraves fire engine above is Sugar Land's first fire chief, Luke Thompson.

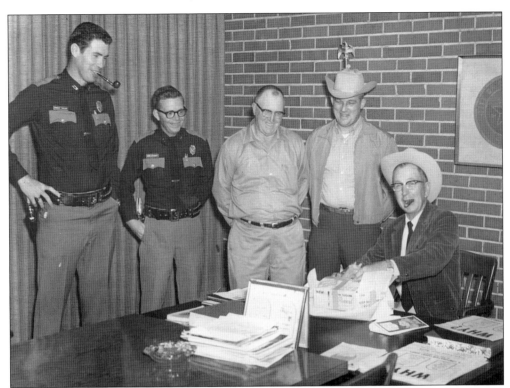

An important step during the 1960s was the creation of a city police force. Sugar Land hired Joe Burke to the newly created position of city marshal. J. E. Fendley (far right) was later hired as Sugar Land's first police chief. Pictured from left to right with the chief during his birthday celebration in 1969 are officers Earnest Taylor, Eber Stewart, animal control officer Tilman Lewis, and officer Larry Ross. Taylor, Stewart, and Ross were the first officers hired by Fendley. (Chief Earnest Taylor.)

Hired in 1969, officer Earnest Taylor learned police work on the job, advancing from patrol officer to detective to captain of the Fort Bend Major Crimes Task Force to assistant chief and finally to police chief in 1992. He retired in 2003. Taylor is pictured in 1970 next to one of the department's first patrol cars, a 1968 model sedan with a police package. (Chief Earnest Taylor.)

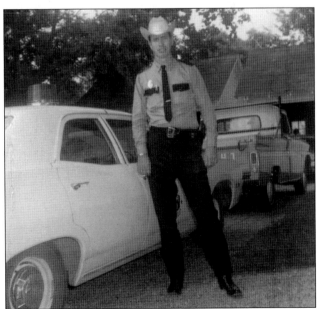

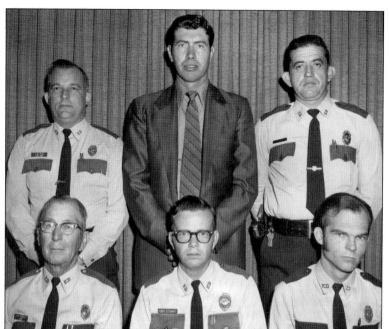

By 1973, the Sugar Land Police Department had grown to six officers. Pictured here from left to right are (first row) Chief J. E. Fendley, officer Eber Stewart, and officer Ken Czarneski; (second row) Assistant Chief Larry Ross, detective Earnest Taylor, and officer Bob Tollett. (Chief Earnest Taylor.)

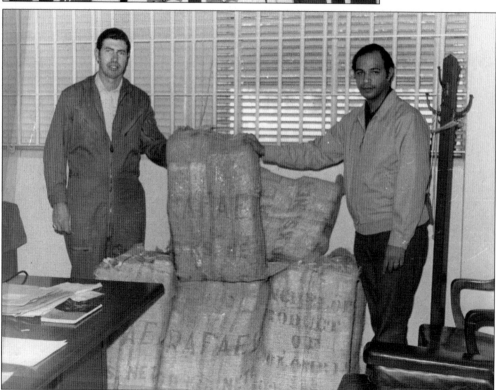

The Fort Bend County Major Crimes Task Force was created during the early 1970s. Earnest Taylor (left) the Sugar Land Police Department captain, was the group's commander for nine years, during which time the group conducted regional undercover and surveillance operations that resulted in major arrests. Pictured with Taylor is officer Joe Prejan. (Chief Earnest Taylor.)

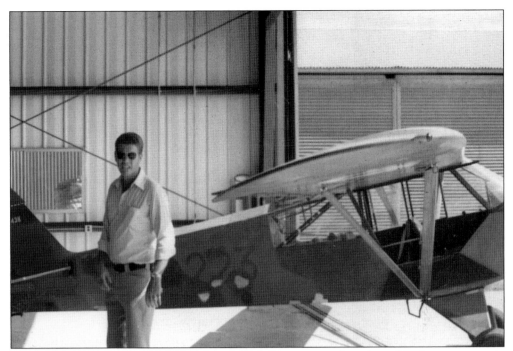

In 1979, the Fort Bend County Major Crimes Task Force acquired a military L21B reconnaissance plane. Dr. Don "Doc" Hull helped Sugar Land Police Department captain Earnest Taylor (pictured) restore the plane to flying condition. Taylor flew the plane, which was the first plane owned and operated by law enforcement in the county, on numerous search and rescue and surveillance operations. (Chief Earnest Taylor.)

Students at Lakeview Elementary School recognized Chief J. E. Fendley and his department for their service to the city during Thanksgiving 1976. Fendley served Sugar Land from his appointment as the first police chief until his retirement in 1982. Assistant Chief Larry Ross was promoted to replace Fendley. (Chief Earnest Taylor.)

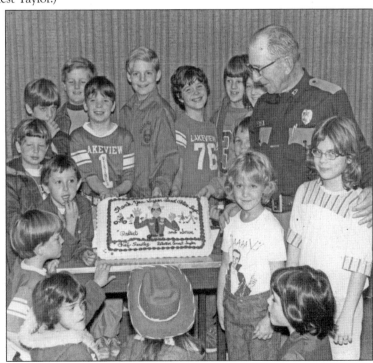

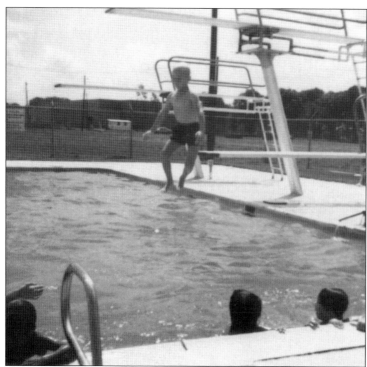

City founders had the foresight to provide park space. Lands donated by Imperial Sugar eventually become Baker Field Park, or just City Park, which eventually included this popular pool. Fred Baker led the Fort Bend Little League (later known as Sugar Land Little League), and the back of his vehicle was used as a concession stand during games.

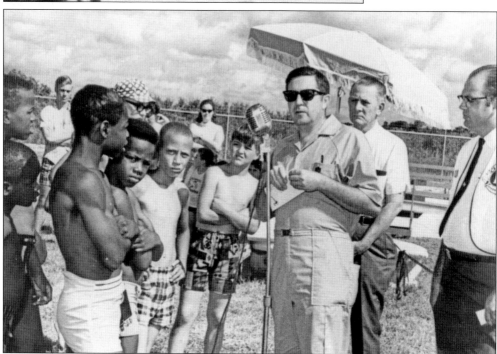

A pool was added in 1966 and opened the following summer, marking the beginning of city recreation in Sugar Land. It was a project made possible by the Sugar Land Lion's Club and the Kempner Foundation. Pictured on opening day are, from left to right, Lion's member Vic Novasad, Fort Bend County Judge Josh Gates, and Lion's member Carl Key. (Vic and Maurice Novasad.)

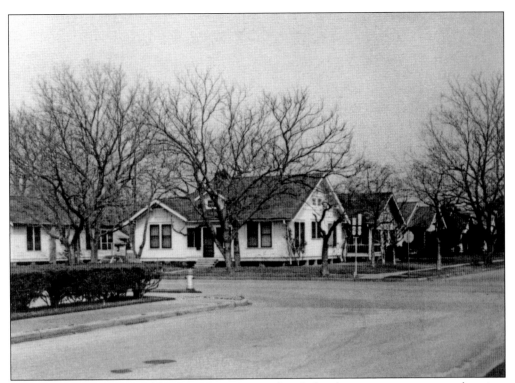

The sugar company provided for the town's every need, including housing, water, sewage, education, medical services, and more. The company even provided electrical and natural gas systems, though these utilities were sold prior to the city's incorporation. (T. C. and Marjorie Rozelle.)

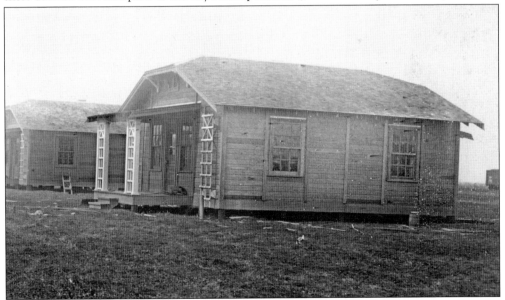

During the early 1960s, Sugar Land City Council obtained an urban renewal project from the Federal Housing Administration. Loans backed by Imperial Sugar enabled the removal of rundown houses to clear the way for newer homes with indoor plumbing. The project led to the growth of areas like Mayfield Park.

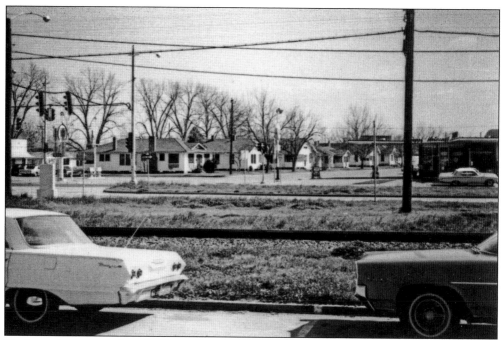

Trash service was another challenge. Residents of the company town were accustomed to trash service five days per week, a service historically provided by the company. A reduction to twice per week was just part of the city's new service level provided to residents. The greater challenge was explaining to citizens that the city's new contractor would not enter homes to remove trash. (T. C. and Marjorie Rozelle.)

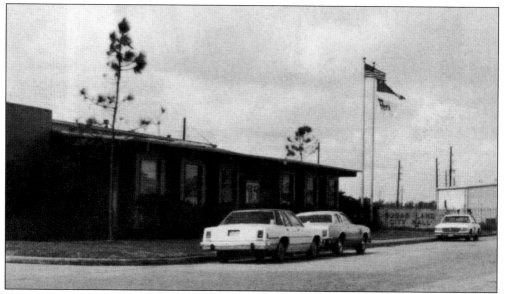

Out of five city halls, this building on Matlage Way served as Sugar Land's third for nearly 20 years. A former hardware store and garden center, the building was deeded to the city from Sugarland Industries in 1973. It was converted to house city hall and the community center, which still remains. Fire Station No. 1 was added later. In December 1993, city hall moved to its fourth location on Corporate Drive.

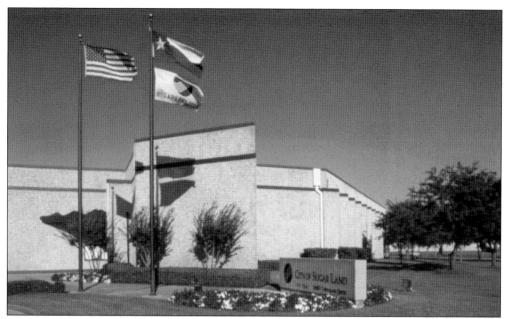

Sugar Land's fourth city hall was located in the Sugar Land Business Park. Extensive renovations were completed prior to the building's grand opening as city hall in 1993. Originally intended as a temporary city hall, the building served as the city's center of government until 2004.

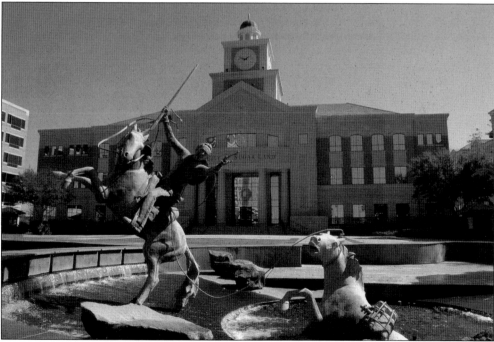

Sugar Land City Hall opened in Sugar Land Town Square on November 22, 2004. This facility allowed the consolidation of city departments into the geographic center of Sugar Land. City hall became the focus of a town square development that essentially created a downtown environment with a 1.2-acre public plaza that accommodates community-wide events and provides a gathering place for residents and visitors.

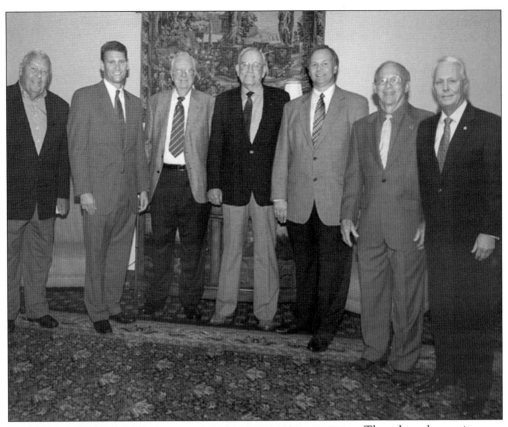

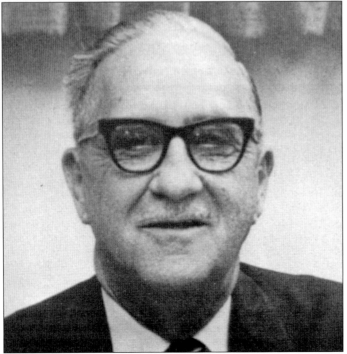

There have been nine mayors in Sugar Land's history. Pictured here in this group photograph above are, from left to right, Bill Little (1961–1965), David G. Wallace (2002–2008), Walter McMeans (1981–1986), Roy Cordes Sr., (1972–1981), Dean A. Hrbacek (1996–2002), Lee Duggan (1986–1996), and James A. Thompson (2008–present). Pictured at left is the late C. E. McFadden (1968–1972). Not pictured here, but seen at the beginning of this chapter, is Sugar Land's first mayor, the late T. E. Harman who served 1959–1961 and 1965–1968.

Eight

Country Club Living in the Suburbs

The extension of the Southwest Freeway to Sugar Land cleared the way for the growth of residential development during the 1960s. The state's highway project extended the freeway through rice fields in Sharpstown to U.S. Highway 90A, a milestone that spurred the development of Sugar Creek and other areas. The Fort Bend Cattle Company sold about 1,200 acres to a developer to create what became Sugar Creek in 1968. The area's first master-planned community introduced country club living near Sugar Land.

Prior to the development of Sugar Creek, the Kempner family set the stage for upscale residential communities in Sugar Land with the development of Venetian Estates. Canals were dredged on family-owned farmland and swamp to build the neighborhood. The development served several purposes by providing new waterside homes, the elimination of a swampy area inhabited by alligators, and continued flood control protection.

Sugar Land and Venetian Estates greatly benefited from the extension of the Southwest Freeway, which improved access and sparked renewed interest in the rural neighborhoods. Also during the early 1960s, a new subdivision development called Imperial Estates, and later Covington Woods, introduced contemporary affordable housing in Sugar Land for the first time. Based on the success of Covington Woods, Venetian Estates, and Sugar Creek, developers began looking for new opportunities in the Sugar Land area. In 1972, the Kempner family sold 7,500 acres to Gerald Hines Interests for the development of First Colony. It was one of the largest land sales in Texas history. Development began in 1977 by Sugarland Properties, Inc. and would follow for the next 30 years. The master-planned community offered home buyers formal landscaping, neighborhoods separated by price range, extensive greenbelts, a golf course and country club, lakes, boulevards, neighborhood amenities, and shopping.

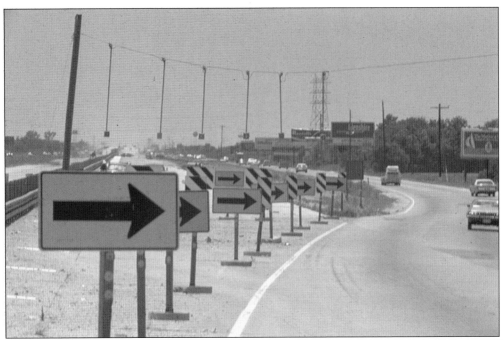

In 1967, more than 206 acres were acquired for the extension of U.S. Highway 59 from the city of Houston into Sugar Land. At that time, the freeway lanes ended at Bissonnet, with only access roads reaching Sugar Land. Through much of the 1960s, the primary route to Sugar Land for motorists was U.S. Highway 90A. The expansion of U.S. Highway 59 facilitated the development of the Sugar Land area's first master-planned community, Sugar Creek. (Don L. Russell.)

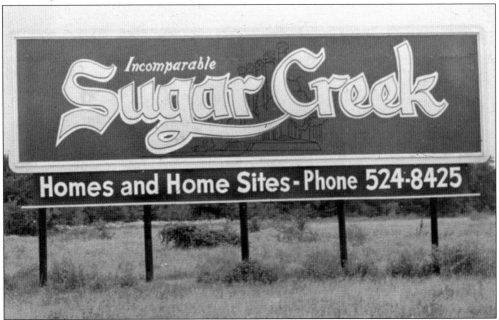

Jack Kamin, the developer of the very successful Nassau Bay, purchased 1,200 acres from the former Fort Bend Cattle Company, and in 1968, he began the development of Sugar Creek, a community that revolved around a golf course and country club. (Don L. Russell.)

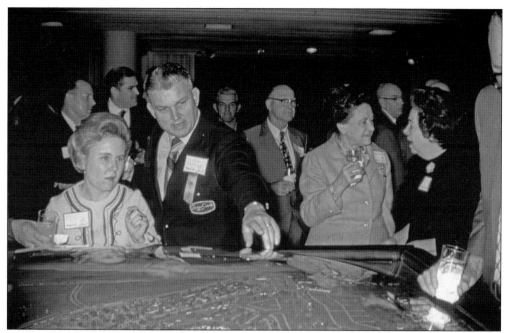

Jack Kamin and a member of the Kempner family reached an agreement for the acreage over coffee in a shop in Clear Lake. Terms were listed on a paper napkin, signed and sealed with a handshake. In 1969, the new project was introduced to prospective buyers by Kamin's partner, Don Russell (pictured), at the Houston Club in downtown Houston. (Don L. Russell.)

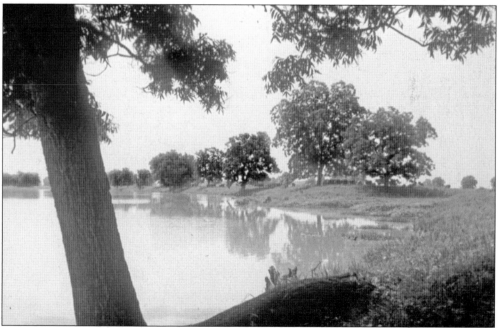

The lands of Sugar Creek had been used for a variety of purposes, including sugarcane, pecan orchards, and cattle. It was also known as the best bird hunting in the county. The Fort Bend Cattle Company realized it could no longer make a profit growing and selling beef in the years prior to the land's sale in 1969. (Don L. Russell.)

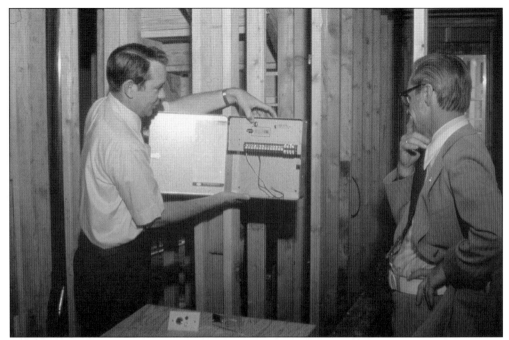

The plan for Sugar Creek called for a highly secure gated community. A NASA employee whose division was responsible for life support during the moon mission was hired to implement an untried security concept: wiring the community so that homes could be monitored from a central facility coordinating police, fire, and emergency medical services. (Don L. Russell.)

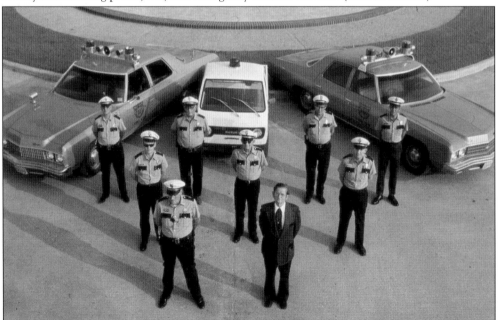

Because Sugar Creek was an unincorporated area in the county, developers employed a separate security force. Around-the-clock uniformed personnel patrolled in marked vehicles. The force included licensed peace officers, and the security company was authorized by the state. (Don L. Russell.)

The distinctive entrance to Sugar Creek includes dramatic imagery comprised of a reflection pool leading to five stately columns. The architecture was part of the historic 1898 Galveston County Courthouse, which weathered the Hurricane of 1900—the worst natural disaster in U.S. history with an estimated 10,000 casualties. The columns were brought to Sugar Creek after the closure of the famous building in 1966. (Don L. Russell.)

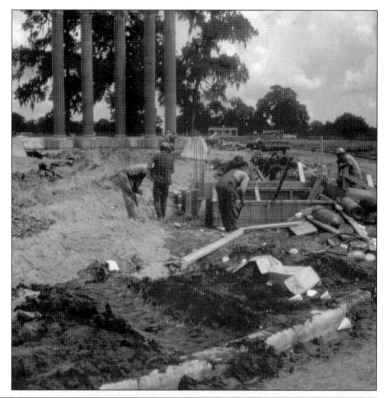

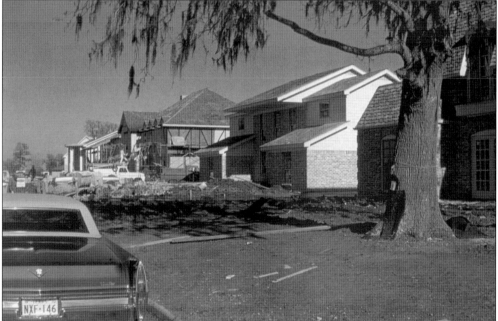

Sugar Creek's first Parade of Homes event included 10 houses that totaled a combined sales price of more than $1 million. In addition to the latest technological security features, families were attracted to a rural, country club lifestyle that included golfing, tennis, and the natural beauty of the new community. (Don L. Russell.)

103

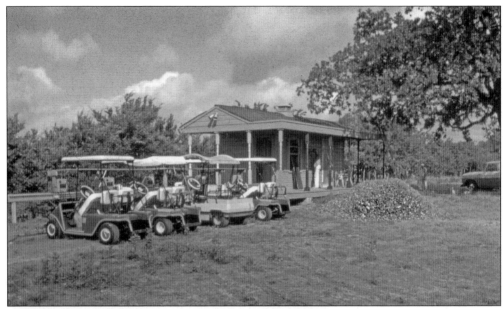

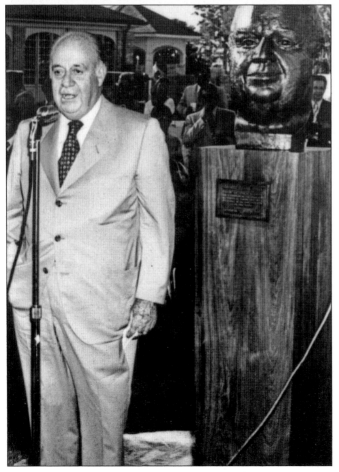

The sales office above became the interim clubhouse and was placed on the bluff where today's clubhouse now stands. The club's founders commissioned legendary golf course architect Robert Trent Jones to design and construct a championship golf course. The first nine holes were completed in 1971. The June 24, 1972, photograph below marked a memorable event. A bronze bust of Robert Trent Jones was unveiled near the putting green. He had designed hundreds of the world's most notable golf courses, including elite courses in Houston. When asked if his course would be the best in Houston, he replied, "No . . . But there will be none finer." (Don L. Russell.)

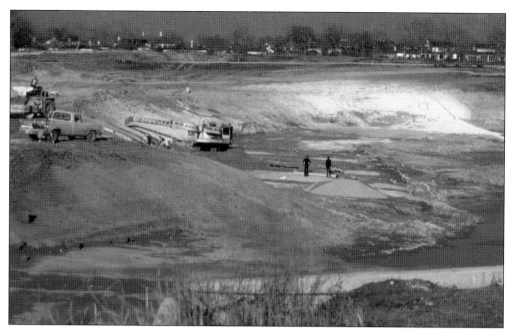

The old cattle watering creek bisecting the first fairway was rerouted underground as lakes were carved and fairways were contoured. The original greens were constructed with only gravel, peat moss, and sand, while grass grew later. Lakes were formed for retention with substantial flood gates installed to address flooding concerns from heavy rains and Brazos River backflow. Plans successfully alleviated flooding and removed it from the floodplain. (Don L. Russell.)

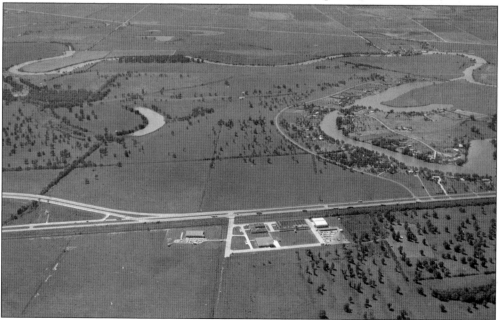

Sugarland Industries sold 7,500 acres to Gerald Hines Interests in 1972 for the development of First Colony—a new master-planned community that would later include extensive greenbelts, a golf course and country club, lakes, boulevards, neighborhood amenities, and shopping. It was one of the largest land sales in Texas history. (Planned Community Developers.)

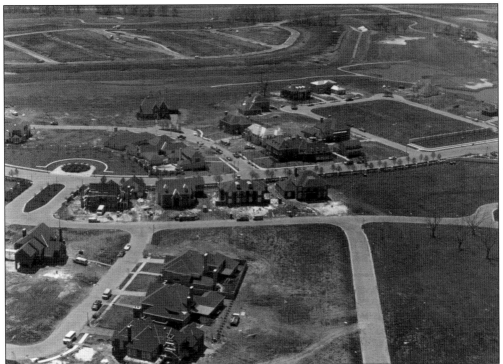

Development began in 1977 by Sugarland Properties, Inc. and would follow for the next 30 years. The master-planned community offered prospective buyers neighborhoods divided by price range. An additional 1,800 acres were acquired in 1981, expanding the total First Colony acreage to 9,300. (Planned Community Developers.)

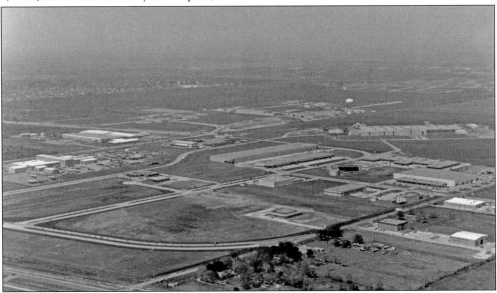

The project's vision included four cornerstones: the 770-acre Sugar Land Office Park, the 1,000-acre Sugar Land Business Park, the 275-acre Town Center anchored by a regional shopping mall, and a broad spectrum of residential neighborhoods. Pictured is an early view of the Sugar Land Business Park. (Planned Community Developers.)

In the course of a single decade, the development already included a vital business and residential community that was home to more than 20,000 people. Leading companies such as Texas Commerce Bank–Sugar Land, Fluor Corporation, the Memorial Hospital System, and others had major facilities at the Sugar Land Office Park. Pictured is the Fluor Corporation, one of Sugar Land's first major corporate citizens.

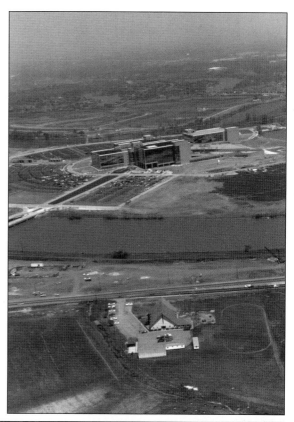

By 1986, Hines's vision for 15 square miles out on the prairie materialized into 34 neighborhoods with 6,500 homes ranging from $50,000 to more than $1 million. Sweetwater Country Club became a fixture of the community, with surrounding neighborhoods home to celebrities and athletes. The golf course became well known throughout the region and was home to the LPGA.

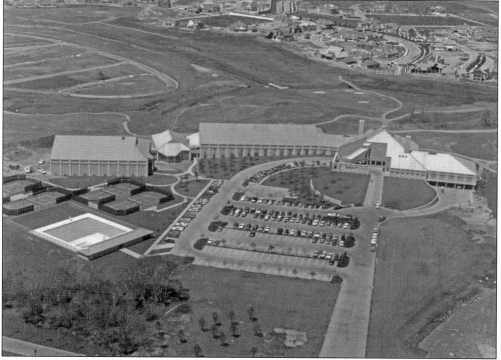

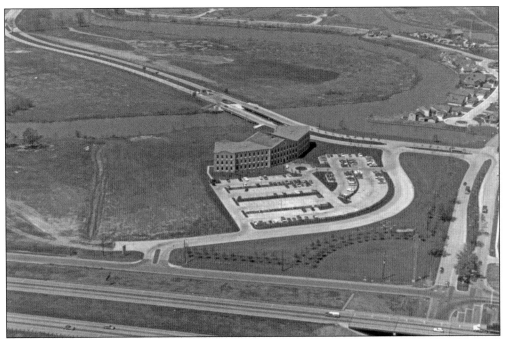

First Colony included corporate headquarters, major office centers, a business park, thousands of new trees, and 150 acres of greenbelts and lakes. Many of the lakes not only created waterfront property, but also helped prevent flooding. An example is Sugar Lakes, pictured in early development.

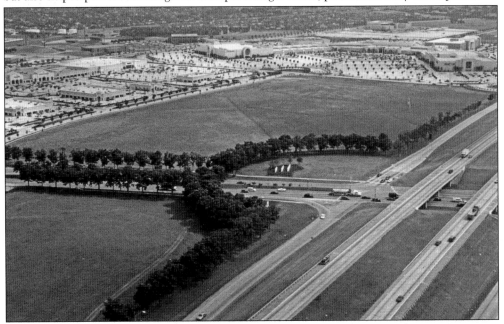

The successful development of First Colony had already contributed to Fort Bend County's position as the fastest-growing county in the country despite the recession of the 1980s. First Colony has since grown into a 9,700-acre master-planned community with a population of approximately 60,000 in just under 16,000 homes, served by over 7 million square feet of commercial and retail space. Pictured is the Town Center site with the First Colony Mall (upper right).

Nine

From Grass Runway to Corporate Airport

Aviation has a storied history in Sugar Land dating back to at least 1953, when Dr. Don "Doc" Hull and his wife, Jenny, founded Hull Field. Hull came to Texas in 1949 to teach oral surgery at the University of Texas at Houston and start a private practice. He also created a dental program, from scratch, for the Texas Department of Corrections (TDC) Southern Region's 17 prisons using old donated equipment from the Galveston County Hospital. He was sole dentist of these prisons for 18 years.

Hull learned to fly in Georgia as a boy. He held a commercial pilot license with flight instructor ratings as well as aircraft mechanics licenses. Airplanes were his passion, and he enjoyed teaching flying lessons and restoring aircraft. He purchased property near Sugar Land in 1953 for an airport and opened Hull Field. Hull Aviation was established, and numerous businesses catering to pilots were offered at the airport.

A typical day for Hull included dental surgery in the morning, aircraft restoration and flight instruction in the afternoon, and more dentistry in the evening at one of the prisons.

The Hulls later rebuilt and extended the runway to 8,000 feet, making it comparable to any in the region. Hull Field was ready to compete with any municipal airport for corporate business and became the primary factor in the Flour Corporation's and the Kansas-Nebraska Pipeline Company's decisions to construct their corporate facilities in Sugar Land.

After years of improvements intended to attract the corporate aviation market, the city purchased the airport in 1990. It was renamed Sugar Land Municipal Airport and later Sugar Land Regional Airport. Following in the steps of Hull, Sugar Land continued investing in the airport to capitalize on the corporate market.

The airport contributes greatly to the local economy by providing jobs, corporate access to local markets, air transportation services, and facilities to house corporate aviation departments. More than a hundred Fortune 500 companies use the airport annually. In 2009 and 2010, Sugar Land Regional Airport was rated the nation's best airport operator by *Aviation International News*, improving from fifth place in previous years.

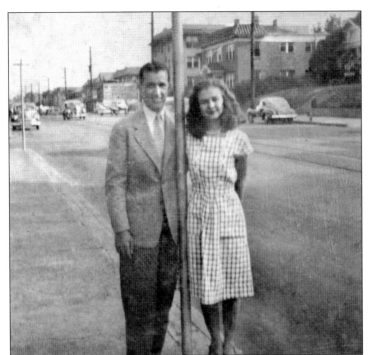

Doc and Jenny Hull met in Georgia where they both worked at the post office. Doc was also studying dentistry at Emory University. The two were married on the ABC *Bride and Groom* radio show in Los Angeles. Doc completed a residency in oral surgery and accepted a teaching fellowship at the University of Texas Dental School in Houston, Texas, before moving to Houston in 1949. (The Hull family.)

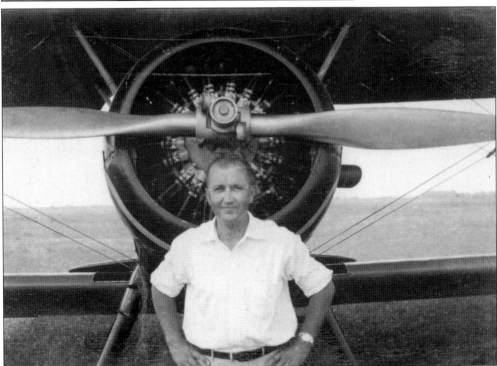

Hull flew out of South Houston Airport and Sam Houston Airport, which both closed in the early 1950s to make way for development. This prompted Hull to look for a place to build an airport that would never close. He located landlocked property for sale adjacent to the TDC Central Prison near Sugar Land and purchased it with a loan from a friend. (The Hull family.)

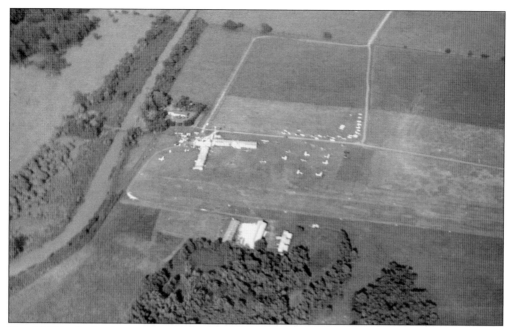

Doc Hull built the first runway with a borrowed motor grader and founded Hull Field in 1953. He obtained access to the property using the main entrance of the prison thanks to his good relationship with TDC. (The Hull family.)

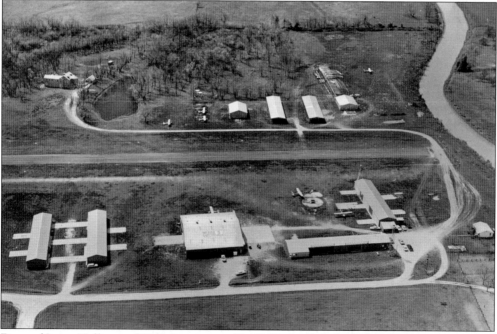

Doc and Jenny Hull started Hull Aviation, and by 1965, it included a flight school, air taxi service, and aircraft rentals, sales, maintenance, painting, and overhaul. Doc also served as the regional Federal Aviation Administration examiner and gave flight tests and licenses to pilots. Doc ran these businesses while maintaining his dental practice, the TDC dental work, and attaining the rank of colonel in the U.S. Army Reserves. (The Hull family.)

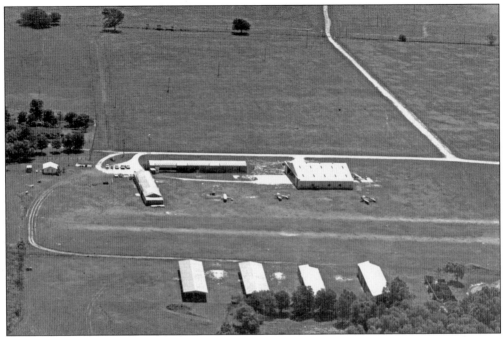

Hull Field never saw a year go by without improvements to the airport. In 1960, a new maintenance hangar facility was completed. The following year it provided refuge from Hurricane Carla for the Hull family when their children—Gail, Donna, and John—slept in an aircraft stored in the hangar during the storm. Everything but the new hangar and the family home was destroyed, so Don and Jenny Hull rebuilt the airport and added new hangars. A new 3,200-foot paved runway was built in 1962, one of the first runway improvements that would lay the groundwork for development as the region's premier corporate facility. (The Hull family.)

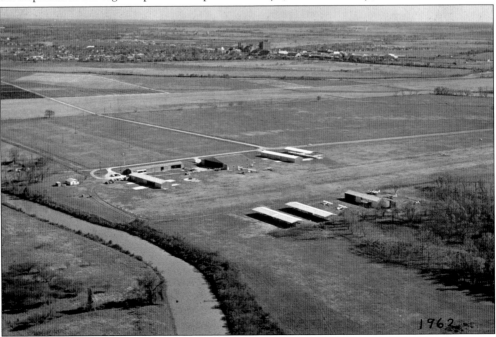

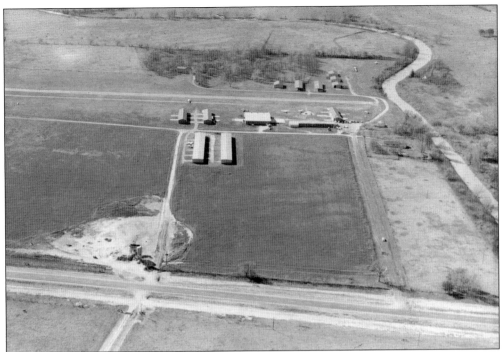

Hull donated land to the State of Texas for highway right-of-way, and Texas State Highway 6 was built in 1968, providing excellent access to the airport. This visionary move ensured that critical infrastructure existed to accommodate future aviation businesses. (The Hull family.)

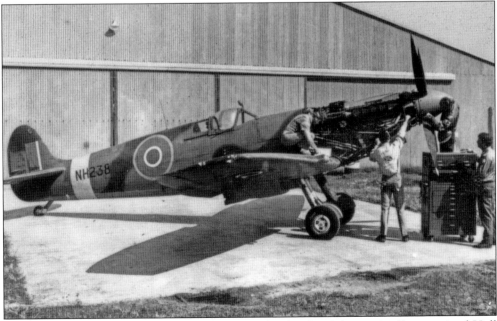

Restoration of military aircraft, including some for the Confederate Air Force, gained Hull recognition throughout the region. His expertise caught the attention of many astronauts who were members of a flying club that regularly traveled to Hull Field. The astronauts helped Hull find parts for his planes in exchange for flight time in the vintage war planes. (The Hull family.)

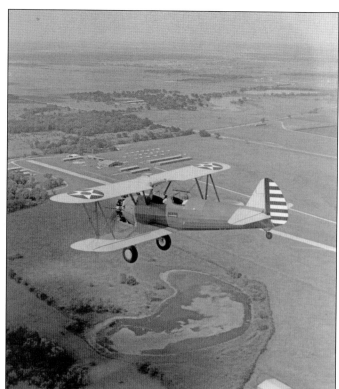

Pictured flying above Hull Field in a renovated Stearman biplane are Hull and his son, John. The photograph was taken by astronaut Stuart "Stu" Roosa, who was the command module pilot for the Apollo 14 moon mission, and space shuttle commander Joe Engle. The Stearman was built in the United States during the 1930s and 1940s as a military trainer aircraft. (The Hull family.)

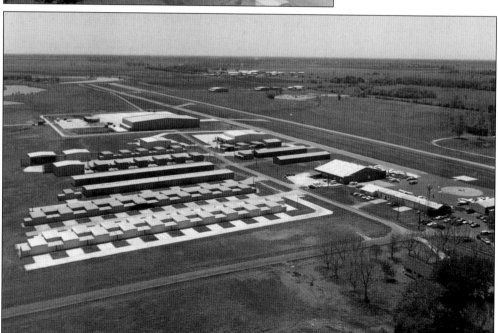

The Hull family built one of the largest flight schools in the state of Texas, operating it until the 1970s, when it was purchased by renowned aviator Maybelle Fletcher and her husband. The Fletcher family ran the school for another 25 years, making it the oldest flight school in Texas. (The Hull family.)

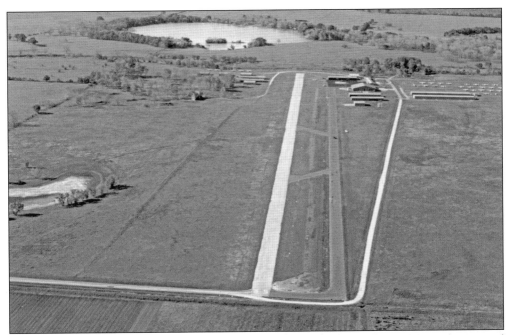

Realizing that attracting corporate aircraft was necessary for the airport to survive the ups and downs of the economy, Doc Hull completed a land trade with the Texas Department of Corrections in 1977 and extended the runway from 3,200 feet to 4,475 feet. Corporate jets began to use the facility. (The Hull family.)

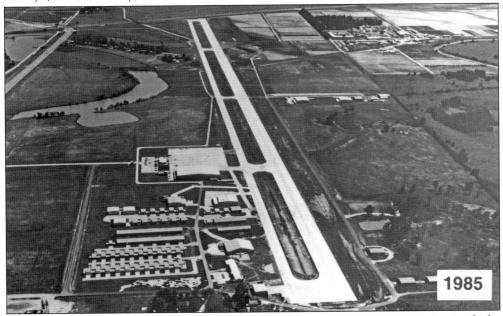

In 1980, Hull's son, John, joined the operation full time, and they began negotiations with the prison system and the state to purchase land for expansion. In 1985, the Hulls completed the purchase of 110 acres. The runway and taxiway were rebuilt to 8,000 feet, accommodating jets as large as 737s. The new runway included a state-of-the-art instrument landing system and a high-intensity lighting system, all still in use today. (The Hull family.)

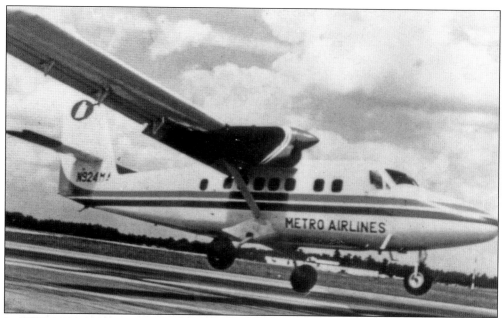

In 1983, a new passenger terminal and corporate hangar were constructed to further focus on corporate aviation. Eastern Airlines remodeled the original terminal and started the Eastern Metro Express shuttle to George Bush Intercontinental Airport with 19 flights a day. Commercial airline service has since been discontinued at the airport to allow the city to more favorably compete for federal funding. (The Hull family.)

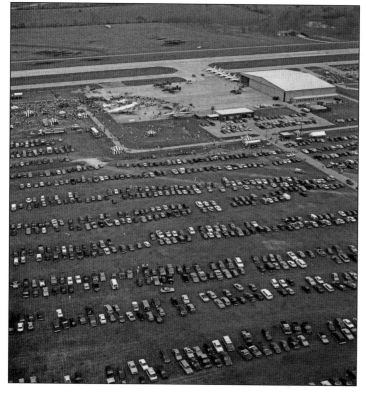

Astronauts frequently visited Hull Field, including Deke Slayton, one of NASA's original Mercury 7 astronauts, who participated in one of the aviation races held as part of the airport's annual air show. Slayton lost a propeller in the race but skillfully landed his aircraft, an impressive dead-stick landing that was never documented for posterity. Among the aviators racing was former astronaut Robert "Hoot" Gibson, who flew five space shuttle missions. (The Hull family.)

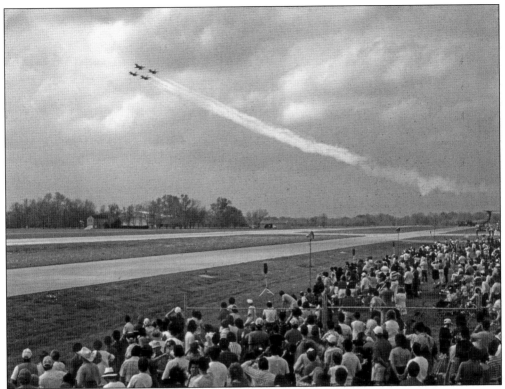

In 1989, the U.S. Air Force Thunderbirds performed at Hull Field's annual show—a first for a privately owned airport. The air demonstration squadron, based at Nellis Air Force Base in Las Vegas, Nevada, performed aerobatic formations and solo flying in specially marked U.S. Air Force jet aircraft for a capacity crowd at Hull Field. (The Hull family.)

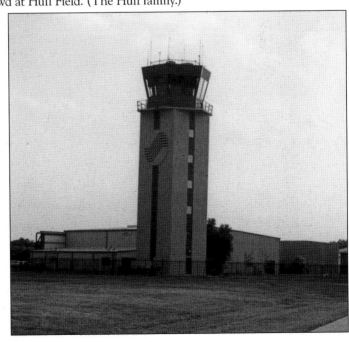

A state-of-the-art air traffic control tower was officially dedicated in 2001. As part of the festivities, former astronaut Gene Cernan, the last man to walk on the moon, was the first man to officially land at Sugar Land Regional Airport with the assistance of Federal Aviation Administration controllers in the new tower. (The Hull family.)

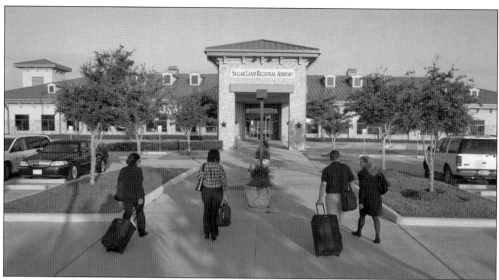

In October 2002, Sugar Land Regional Municipal Airport unveiled a new name: Sugar Land Regional Airport (SLRA). A new 20,000-square-foot terminal opened in 2006 that included a full-service fixed-base operator (FBO), crew suite, executive lounge, conference rooms, retail shops, aircraft repair, avionics sales, flight school, and car rental facilities. The terminal was followed by a new 60-acre T-hangar complex in 2009 and a U.S. Customs facility for international travelers. (The Hull family.)

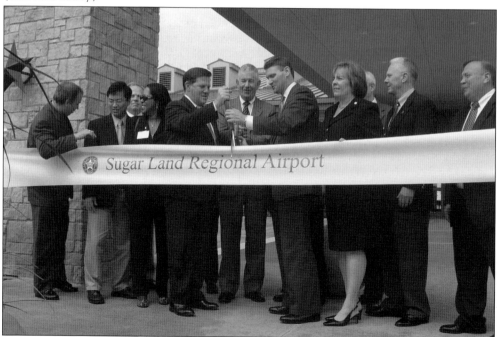

Sugar Land Regional Airport's new terminal opened with great fanfare. Pictured with former U.S. House Majority Leader Tom DeLay and former Sugar Land mayor David Wallace were members of Sugar Land City Council and Texas aviation officials. In 2009 and 2010, *Aviation International News* named SLRA the best FBO in the Americas. More than a hundred Fortune 500 companies utilize the airport annually. (The Hull family.)

Ten

MODERN HISTORY

Sugar Land was incorporated in 1959 with a population of 2,259 and had grown to 84,511 by 2010. On January 17, 1981, voters approved a mayor-council government, investing all powers of the city in a council composed of a mayor and five council members. On August 9, 1986, voters approved a "council-manager" form of government, providing a city manager to serve as chief administrative officer.

Sugar Land began attracting the attention of major corporations throughout the 1980s. Schlumberger, Unocal, and others offered their employees the opportunity to work within minutes of their home. The master-planned community of Sugar Creek was annexed into Sugar Land during 1984, setting the stage for the much larger annexation of First Colony during the 1990s.

A portion of the 1974 movie *The Sugarland Express* is set in Sugar Land. The first feature film directed by Steven Spielberg, many of the movie's earliest scenes were filmed at nearby Beauford H. Jester Prison and Richmond, Texas; ironically, none of it was shot in Sugar Land.

The 2000 U.S. Census showed that Sugar Land had grown 158 percent in 10 years, making it Texas's second-fastest growing city in the 1990s.

The Imperial Sugar refinery closed in 2002, though the company maintains its corporate headquarters in Sugar Land. *Money* magazine and CNN/Money ranked Sugar Land the third-best place to live in America in 2006. In 2007, CQ Press ranked Sugar Land fifth on its list of the safest cities in the United States.

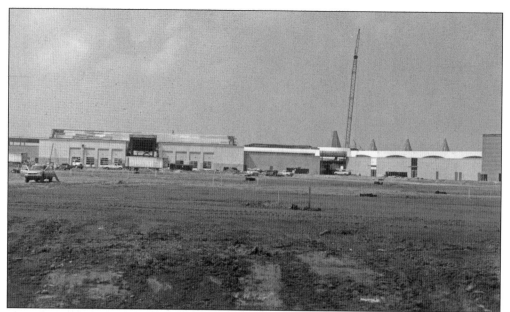

One of Sugar Land's first major public-private developments, the opening of First Colony Mall in 1996 was the result of more than a decade of planning and vision. The opening of the mall created strong sales tax revenue that offset residential property taxes.

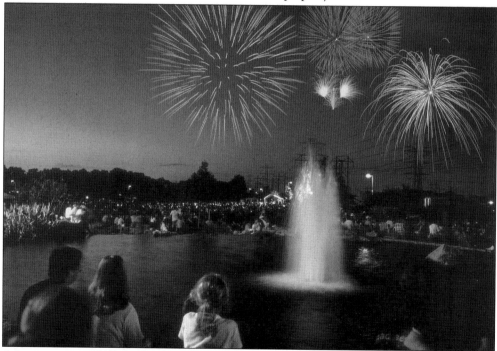

A barren source of fill dirt bounded by a utility easement became a source of community pride after opening on July 4, 2000. Used mainly for excavation, city planners saw the 110 acres as a diamond in the rough. Oyster Creek, home to small picnics and events attracting over 50,000 people, joins other major local parks including City Park, Imperial, Eldridge, Lost Creek, Memorial Park, and the Brazos River Corridor.

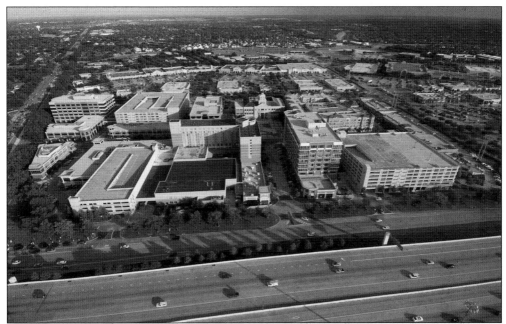

While many cities have revitalized their downtowns, Sugar Land created one where none existed before. A product of more than a decade of planning, Sugar Land Town Square was designed to include business, retail, entertainment, and living in one central hub. It included 300,000 square feet of Class A office space, 200,000 square feet of retail space, more than 160 condominiums, the county's first four-star hotel and conference center, and city hall.

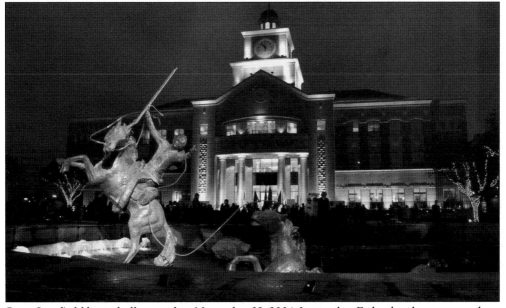

Sugar Land's fifth city hall opened on November 22, 2004. Its timeless Federal architecture anchors Sugar Land Town Square. The facility allowed the consolidation of city departments into the geographic center of Sugar Land. Designed to bring community and business together, the wide plaza and historic fountain created a downtown environment and provided a central and popular gathering place—a heart for the community.

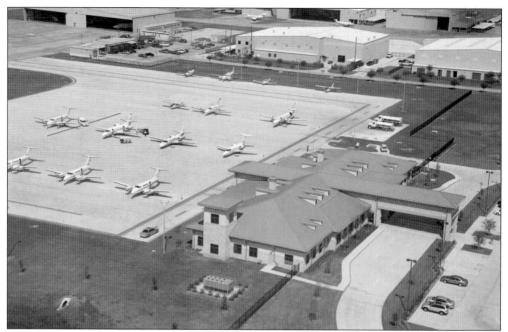

From grass runway to modern, luxury corporate airport, Sugar Land Regional Airport has distinguished itself as a premier facility from local to international circles. An important part of the regional economy, it provides jobs, international corporate access to local markets, air transportation services, and outstanding facilities to house corporate aviation departments. In 2009 and 2010, *Aviation International News* named SLRA the best fixed-base operator in the entire Western Hemisphere.

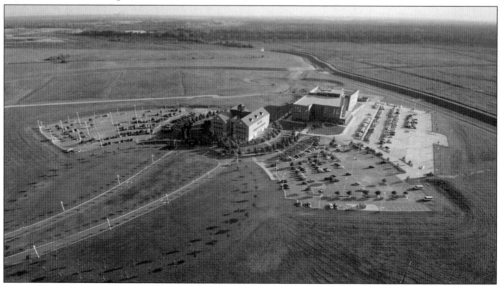

City officials approached the state in 1997 for a land donation, and the Texas Legislature subsequently deeded more than 660 acres for a university and park development—the first time a Texas State Legislature deeded land to a municipality. The city provided more than $7 million for construction. The goal was to expand college-level education and ensure a qualified labor force for businesses.

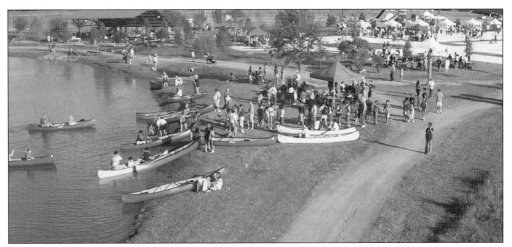

The city acquired approximately 1,200 acres of land along the banks of the Brazos River for parks, open space, and conservation. The first 420 acres were opened as Memorial Park on November 10, 2007, part of a planned 3,600-acre parkland development. Memorial Park added to the city's more than 18 neighborhood and community parks totaling 771 acres.

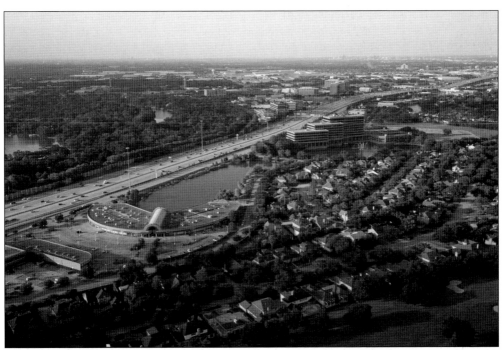

During the first decade of the 21st century, more than half a billion dollars of highway projects in Sugar Land were completed, many of which were finished ahead of schedule due to state and federal partnerships with active participation from the city. Major corridors including U.S. Highway 59, State Highway 6, and U.S. Highway 90A provided important infrastructure to support one of the region's strongest economies.

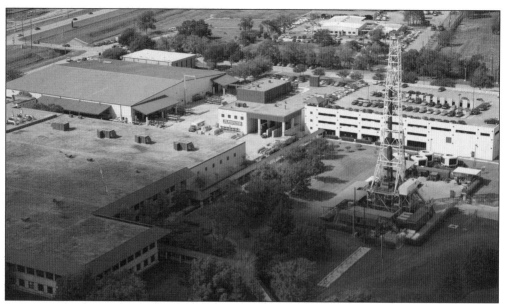

Businesses calling Sugar Land home are as diverse as its population. Ranging from semiconductors to energy, construction, engineering, and research, Sugar Land's economy has grown exponentially, attracting both regional and international firms. With strong transportation corridors, outstanding quality of life, and the internationally recognized Sugar Land Regional Airport, hundreds of businesses, both large and small, have found this an exceptional destination.

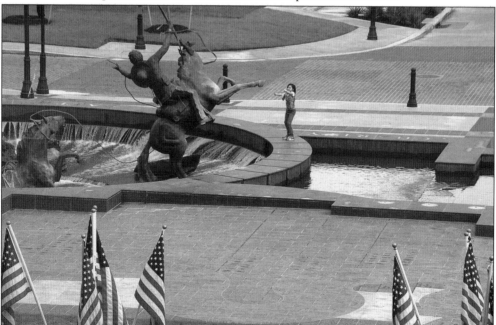

The bedrock of Sugar Land's success is shaped by values the community holds dear, values proudly etched into the city's public plaza for all to see: commerce, community, family, education, charity, faith, and hope. Sugar Land celebrated its 50th anniversary during 2009, honoring a rich history, dedication to family, mutual understanding and respect, and citizenship—values that set a firm course for the city's future.

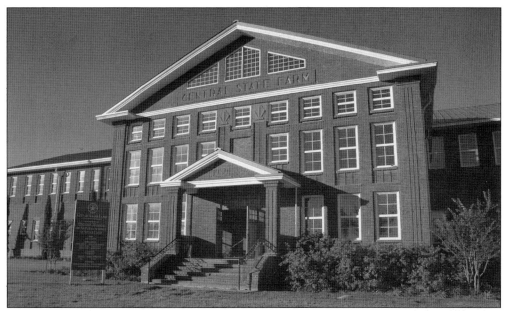

The former dormitory for the Central State Prison Farm, a place of mandatory confinement, reopened as the Sugar Land Museum of Natural Science on October 3, 2009. The project was the result of a partnership between the city, the Houston Museum of Natural Science, and developer Newland Communities. The museum was the first step toward fulfilling the community's need for a cultural/entertainment district.

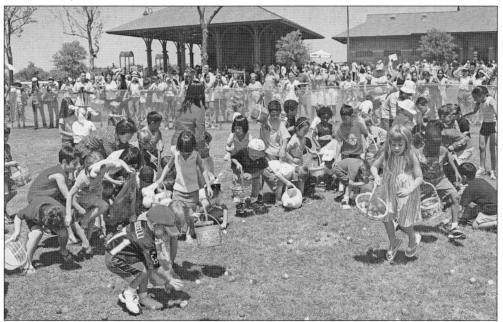

Record growth through the 1980s and 1990s resulted in changing demographics. By 2010, Sugar Land held the distinction as one the nation's most diverse cities, with an Asian community representing nearly 30 percent of the city's population. Two years after becoming the nation's first "Community of Respect," Sugar Land was recognized by the Anti-Defamation League for the third straight year in 2010 for its ongoing commitment to foster an inclusive community.

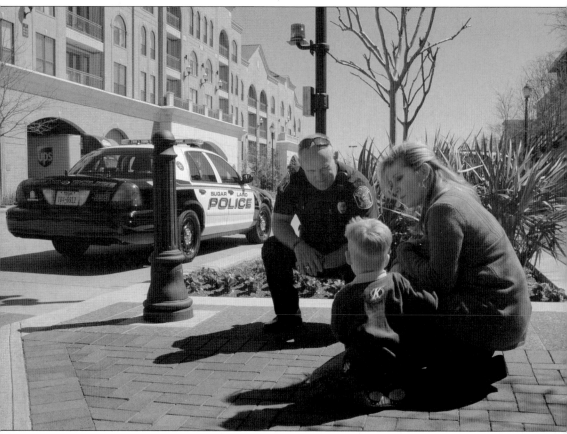

By 2010, the Sugar Land Police Department had grown from four employees in 1969 to 176 employees dedicated to improving the life of the citizens of Sugar Land by reducing crime and making Sugar Land the safest place to live in the United States. Sugar Land was first named one of America's safest cities in 2007, a distinction based on an analysis of FBI crime statistics.

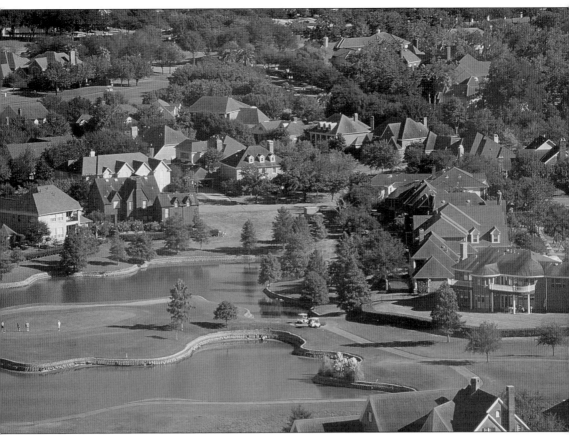

Sugar Land, maintaining a population of around 2,000 through the first half of the 20th century, has grown to a population of 84,511 in 2010. It is known as a community meticulously planned to address the priorities of life: a well-planned, safe city with a thriving economy, first-class recreational facilities, and top-rated schools. These factors contribute to the city's continued growth.

www.arcadiapublishing.com

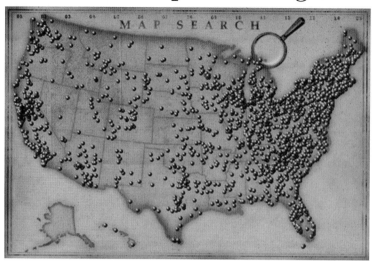

Discover books about the town where you grew up, the cities where your friends and families live, the town where your parents met, or even that retirement spot you've been dreaming about. Our Web site provides history lovers with exclusive deals, advanced notification about new titles, e-mail alerts of author events, and much more.

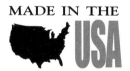

MADE IN THE

Arcadia Publishing, the leading local history publisher in the United States, is committed to making history accessible and meaningful through publishing books that celebrate and preserve the heritage of America's people and places. Consistent with our mission to preserve history on a local level, this book was printed in South Carolina on American-made paper and manufactured entirely in the United States.

This book carries the accredited Forest Stewardship Council (FSC) label and is printed on 100 percent FSC-certified paper. Products carrying the FSC label are independently certified to assure consumers that they come from forests that are managed to meet the social, economic, and ecological needs of present and future generations.

FSC
Mixed Sources
Product group from well-managed forests and other controlled sources

Cert no. SW-COC-001530
www.fsc.org
© 1996 Forest Stewardship Council

Find Your Place in History.